RIVER RAFTING IN CANADA

The author is grateful for a senior grant from the Canada Council.

Cover: Raft plunges through the whitewater of the Batiscan's *Les Trois Roches Rapides* (Three Rock Rapids).

Photographs by Richard Harrington
Cover Design by Sharon Schumacher
Design and Cartography by Robert Chrestensen

Printed in U.S.A.

RIVER RAFTING IN CANADA

Richard Harrington

Alaska Northwest Publishing Company
Edmonds, Washington

Contents

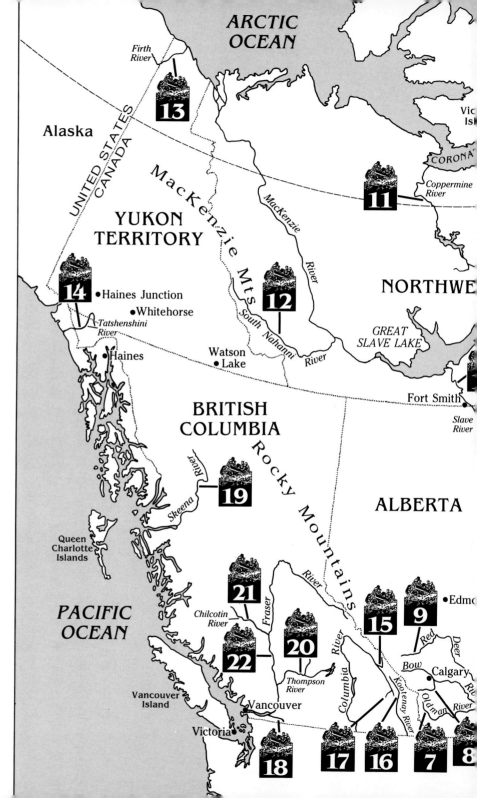

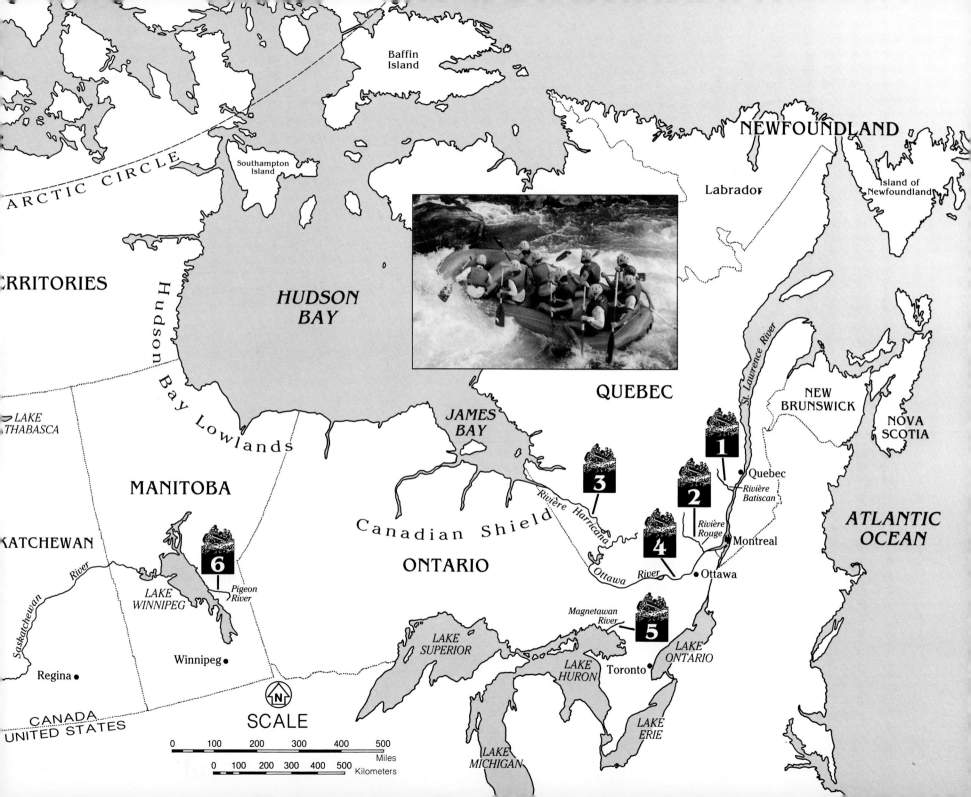

ARCTIC CIRCLE

Baffin
Island

Southampton
Island

NEWFOUNDLAND

Labrador

Island of
Newfoundland

RRITORIES

LAKE
THABASCA

HUDSON
BAY

Hudson Bay

Hudson Bay Lowlands

JAMES
BAY

QUEBEC

St. Lawrence River

NEW
BRUNSWICK

NOVA
SCOTIA

MANITOBA

Canadian Shield

Rivière Harricana

3

2

1

Quebec

Rivière
Batiscan

ATLANTIC
OCEAN

KATCHEWAN

Saskatchewan
River

LAKE
WINNIPEG

6

Pigeon
River

ONTARIO

Ottawa River

4

Rivière
Rouge

Montreal

Ottawa

Winnipeg

Regina

LAKE
SUPERIOR

Magnetawan
River

5

LAKE
ONTARIO

Toronto

CANADA
UNITED STATES

LAKE
HURON

LAKE
MICHIGAN

LAKE
ERIE

N

SCALE

0   100   200   300   400   500
                                    Miles

0   100   200   300   400   500
                                    Kilometers

About River Rafting

Having canoed many Canadian rivers, boated down the Yukon, traveled by barge down the Saskatchewan, and followed many old fur-trade routes, I believed I knew Canadian waterways. In the Antarctic, I had made many wet landings in inflatable rubber boats to photograph penguin colonies and iceberg tunnels.

Then, here in my own country I discovered a couple of dozen rivers via commercial raft trips.

Modern inflatable rafts were developed during World War II, but it was not long before their recreational possibilities were recognized. Thousands of small craft were bought for individual pleasure, though relatively few of them in Canada. Commercial rafts may run up to thirty-eight feet and are capable of carrying thirty passengers through long trains of high waves. Most of those plying Canadian rivers are eighteen to twenty feet, with space for ten to twelve including the boatman, and still draw only four inches.

My first raft trip occurred in British Columbia, which has Canada's foremost rafting rivers. But the adventures in this book are geographical rather than chronological, beginning in the province of Quebec since the Atlantic provinces boast little whitewater.

Wherever water flows the act of creation still goes on, and is seen to good advantage while one is drifting down a river on a raft. Some streams have flowed in

Rating River Difficulty

River difficulty is rated using the six-part International River Classification System. Individual rapid ratings are called classes, while sections are called grades. The rating system for river sections follows. The rapid rating scale is based on the same difficulty levels, but uses Roman numerals. (Class I rapids are not indicated).

Grade 1 — VERY EASY
- ☐ Suitable for novices in all boats.
- ☐ Waves small and regular. Passages clear with occasional channel bars and artificial difficulties such as bridge piers.

Grade 2 — EASY
- ☐ Suitable for Intermediate Open Canoe, Novice Closed Canoe or White Water Boat with intermediate accompaniment.
- ☐ Rapids of medium difficulty, with clear and wide passages. Low ledges, sweepers, snags, log jams and large protruding boulders may be present. Open canoes may ship some water.

Grade 3 — MEDIUM DIFFICULTY
- ☐ Suitable for Advanced Paddlers in Open Canoes and Intermediate Paddlers in White Water and Closed Boats.
- ☐ Waves numerous, high and irregular rocks, eddies and rapids with clear and narrow passages requiring precise maneuvering. Inspection usually needed. Upper limit for open canoes, although extended reaches at this level are not recommended.

Grade 4 — DIFFICULT
- ☐ Suitable for Advanced Paddlers in Closed Canoes and White Water Boats. Not suitable for Open Canoes.
- ☐ Long rapids with powerful and irregular waves. Narrow passages through rocks and boiling eddies, requiring precise maneuvering. Course difficult to reconnoiter from the water. Inspection mandatory.

Grade 5 — VERY DIFFICULT
- ☐ Suitable for Expert White Water Paddlers only.
- ☐ Extremely difficult, long and very violent rapids following each other almost without interruption. Channel bed is extremely obstructed. Big drops, steep gradient and violent current. Inspection essential but may be difficult due to nature of the terrain.

Grade 6 — EXTRAORDINARILY DIFFICULT
- ☐ Suitable for teams of Expert White Water Paddlers, at favorable water levels and with adequate provision for rescue.
- ☐ Difficulties of Grade 5 carried to extremes of navigability. Nearly impossible and very dangerous.

the same trench since prehistoric times, cutting a trough deeper year by year. Others have abandoned their former beds to flow along a new route. History is to be read in the rocks and oxbows.

"The faster the water, the greater the thrills," goes the saying, but safety looms large. Guests enjoy being frightened (like children hearing ghost stories) so long as there is no real danger. Consequently most outfitters insist upon high-buoyancy life jackets and, in rocky water, crash helmets. Paying customers respond with a delicious shiver to scarily named rapids — Jaws of Death, Washing Machine, Hell's Gate.

Just as no two rivers can be identical, no two trips are exactly the same. The hardware may be the same, the guides equally skilled, the scenery unchanged. But the weather varies, as does the water level. The outfitter cannot be blamed for the latter conditions, nor for mosquitoes.

Not every rafting trip is a joyous bounce down some foaming river in brilliant sunshine. The outfitter has a responsibility to be honest in his advertising, not promote fishing when there is none, not con the reader with bombastic phrases of fierce rapids or descriptions of nonexistent wildlife. He has an obligation to provide the food promised and the transportation support, and not to list rivers that he merely *hopes* to run.

Rapids are classified internationally by the rafting associations, from O (flat water) to VI (unrunnable). The rafting community has a vocabulary of its own. When you hear that a river is "very technical" it means that running it requires considerable technique. The upturned snout of a pontoon is termed a *J-tube. Hole* (eddy), *hydraulic* (whirlpool), *haystack* (high-standing wave), *reversal* (back-curling wave), *put-in place,* and *body surfing* are among the many terms.

The search for suitable rivers goes on constantly. Outfitters scan maps and calculate logistics for reaching faraway rivers. Will the lure of a "wild" river, untrammeled by dams, bridges or canals, counterbalance the expense of getting there? Or would it be wiser, more economically viable, to put your rafts on a river close to a large population center?

An outfitter who has pioneered a remote river may feel possessive, but no one can stake a claim to rafting rights. Still, no one muscles in without due courtesy.

Not every commercial outfit, nor every raftable river, is featured in these pages. Outfits do change hands, or shift location. Or a river may dry up, and the vacationist may find his plans left on dry ground. These twenty-odd are rivers I myself have rafted with durable companies. Happy Rafting!

Richard Harrington

General Release and Liability Exclusion

In consideration of (Rafting Company) accepting me on a wilderness adventure trip, as more particularly set out in my application form, and in consideration of other good and valuable consideration, I, the undersigned, understand that the wilderness adventure trip offered by (Rafting Company) involves risks and dangers to my person and property and I hereby accept such risks and dangers.

I hereby waive all rights of legal action I have or may here after have against (Rafting Company), its agents and employees, of and from all manner of claims, demands, damages, actions, or causes of action arising out of the wilderness adventure trip.

For greater certainty, I acknowledge and agree that (Rafting Company) shall not be liable for any costs, expenses, or damages to my person or property howsoever caused, including without limitation, the breach of representations, expressed or implied, accidents, acts of God, negligence of (Rafting Company), its agents or employees, faulty equipment and variations in scheduling.

NAME _____

ADDRESS _____

CITY _____ PROVINCE _____

DATE _____

SIGNATURE _____

NOTE — Adults or guardians must sign for minors (under 16) whether they accompany the minor on the trip or not.

The Canadian Shield

Between the North Atlantic and the vast inland plain called the prairies sprawls an immense region of ancient Precambrian rock. This was once a group of sharp young mountains, hung like a huge collar around Hudson and James bays. Five ice ages wore down the mountains, and glaciers scraped the bedrock bare and smooth.

As the glaciers, two miles thick in places, melted, the land rose and tilted and formed faults and ledges. The retreating glaciers left prehistoric Lake Algonquin, which in time drained to the east. They left behind the Great Lakes and innumerable lesser lakes and ponds. Creeks and rivers linked these waters, which became flowing highways for exploration and the fur trade. Today they provide pleasure for boaters and rafters.

The rivers will flow as long as rain and snow continue to fall, and the forest cover remains as it does in the north of Quebec, Ontario and Manitoba provinces. There the rivers dash to the sea in every direction. They froth and foam in spate (many of them modified by hydroelectric dams), and most shrink in the heat waves of summer. Then you can see the rocks and boulders that create the rapids and swirls and eddies.

Early morning mist rises from the Pigeon, one of the great rivers of the Canadian Shield.

Rivière Batiscan
QUEBEC

At the present time, Rivière Batiscan is the rafting river farthest east in Canada. It rises in Lac Batiscan on the edge of the vast Laurentides Park, west and north of the provincial capital, Quebec City. By curves and kinks it enters and foams through *La Reserve Faunique de Portneuf.*

From Quebec City I drove in the late May sunshine thirty-five miles to the hamlet of *Rivière a Pierre* (Stony River). My being there was a shot in the dark, so to speak, for I had been warned that the one-day trip was fully booked that holiday weekend. Still, it was the only time I had available, and I hoped for at least one no-show.

In the village, the yellow school bus that had been chartered for the occasion filled up with forty-five lively young *Quebecois* chattering French. A head-count showed that all the expected guests had arrived, so I could not float down the Batiscan that day. The bus rolled off to the local base buildings of Nouveau Monde/New World River Expeditions. The base is located just within the portals of the Portneuf Game Reserve.

Since I was particularly concerned with pictures that day, I was instructed to follow the flatbed truck already loaded with five inflated scarlet rafts. The company's photographer could ride with me and guide me to the best vantage point above the first lot of whitewater, *Les Trois Roches* (Three Rock Rapids).

It was fortunate in a way that the two drivers ahead of me knew the way well enough to raise a cloud of dust as they speeded twenty-five miles into the bush alongside the clear, clean Batiscan.

Driving more slowly over the curving, hilly road, I would have eaten dust had I tried to keep up. Henri, beside me, spoke no English but steered me with hand signals. Otherwise I would surely have lost my way.

Finally, Henri indicated a turn over a small bridge. Then we walked a little and drove a jeep two or three miles to the put-in place. It was a colorful scene — whitewater foaming around brown rocks under a sky brilliantly blue, and in the foreground the rafters in form-fitting black wetsuits, sleek as seals, topped by red life jackets and yellow hockey helmets. They mounted their rafts, paddles flashing, and Henri and I scurried to his lookout halfway through the rapids, where he had found the best angle for shots.

Click! went our cameras, click, click, click, as one after another the five rafts bucked and bounced over the crest of *Trois Roches* waves and into the big rollers of *Les Rouleaux.* Even over the noise of the rushing water we could hear shouts and high-pitched squeals.

Henri and I turned back to the base, where he would

Highly visible *(left)* with their red and yellow gear, these rafters are ready to set out on the Batiscan. Guest *(above)* wearing a wetsuit tugs on her waterproof booties.

develop his film and print eight-by-ten photos of each raft riding the waves, and have them ready for sale when the rafters returned.

Back at the base, a young man whose English was better than my French told me about the rest of the run.

"We do twenty-one miles of the most active part of the Batiscan, you know. Lots of small rapids before lunch — those waves you photographed are the best of the morning run. Then after a picnic lunch we run some more *petites rapides* and *La Chute Pierre Antoine*. That's a gorge they run easily at this time of year. Tricky in summer, though. Then the guides may make the run with empty rafts while the passengers walk the port-age trail. When the water gets that low, we know it's nearly the end of our season."

Farther downstream loomed *Les Portes de l'Enfer* (Hell's Gates), six kilometers of heavy rapids — long trains of powerful waves. The *La Tour* section parti-cularly requires a considerable degree of skill in negotiating these rapids.

The one-day trip, an exhilarating day-long event, ends on gravel bars below the whitewater. Then back into the waiting bus to return to the base for drinks and snacks, and an opportunity to purchase those souvenir photos of you and your companions riding the waves of *Trois Roches Rapides*.

FOR FURTHER INFORMATION:

Nouveau Monde/New World River
  Expeditions Co.
5475 Paré, Suite 221
Montreal, Quebec
Canada H4P 1P7
Phone (514) 733-7166
      (800) 361-5033

3

Rivière Rouge
QUEBEC

The most rollicking of more than a dozen short rafting trips I have enjoyed was with the bilingual Nouveau Monde/New World River Expeditions Company of Montreal.

"*Allons!*" (Let's go!). Six rafts pushed out into the clear, dimpled waters of *La Rivière Rouge* as it hurtled down the Laurentian Mountains to join the Ottawa.

It was the last trip of the season, and we fifty-some guests made up the tally of thirteen thousand clients in 1983.

Whitewater rafting is not confined to the Rockies and their outliers. At least five Quebec rivers are providing thrills and excitement for a fast-growing clientele that takes to rafts to bounce down churning rapids and spin through eddies. "The wetter the better" seems to be the motto of the light-hearted groups as they gambol in the waves.

The Nouveau Monde firm started in 1980, operated by Danny Levine and Chris Phelan. They run the rivers Rouge, Jacques Cartier, Batiscan and, out from Calumet Island, the Ottawa.

These are the one- and two-day trips within easy reach of the population centers around Lake Ontario, as well as Montreal and Ottawa. Camping buffs go for Nouveau Monde's Harricana venture, a five-day camping trip through northern wilderness to James Bay.

The shorter trips begin at the end of April, when the freshet is wild and cold. Wetsuits are supplied as "the rig of the day," for the splashes can be chilling. By the end of the season in September, the rivers are lower and the water is warmer. Then one may wear shorts or bathing suit. But always, the plastic helmet and life jacket are de rigueur.

For rafting with the Nouveau Monde, you need bring nothing but a sunny disposition, an eagerness to splash through chutes, and a willingness to admire the lovely

Attentive listeners hear safety instructions.

"En avant!" And more raftloads start off down the Rouge.

forest scenery. But bring a healthy appetite to a hearty buffet meal at the end of the float. Oh yes, and be prepared to belt out voyageur songs, *"En roulant ma boule . . ."*

Thus on a bright September Saturday, we crossed the Ottawa River from Hawkesbury, Ontario, and parked near Kilmar, Quebec. Nouveau Monde owns two hundred fifty acres of private land, where the organization has built a clubhouse. There we transferred to a school bus, and were transported through virgin forest of mixed hardwoods to the put-in place.

Some of the guests had never been in a raft before and were decidedly nervous. The lead guide briefed us in French, then English, on rafting etiquette. The chief instruction was, "Have fun!" Next, "Listen to your boatman's instructions." To make that possible we could choose either a Francophone or an Anglophone crewman.

Most of the guests were young *Canadiens*, a sprinkling of *Canadiennes*, and a handful of oldsters. The French spoken was too fast and too colloquial for the English speakers, full of quips and innuendo we

Mock water fights *(left)* add excitement to the Rouge trip.
Even a man overboard *(above)* is all in fun.

could not grasp. Still, the atmosphere was so merry that we blithely tried out our fractured French. It was a happy, congenial crowd.

"*En avant!*" (forward). Perched on the rounded sides of the raft, we dug paddles into the water. The rafts moved into the river, to be caught by the strong current. A little good-natured splashing went on, and a few feigned collisions.

Rivière Rouge is an ideal river for horseplay, for hilarious silliness, with its various rapids and whirl-pools, none of them vicious. You can't go upstream in a raft, we all knew, but it's fun to try. Again and again, the paddlers defied the laws of physics and attempted to backtrack, particularly in the Washing Machine! They made it to the lip of the drop and were hurled back into the current again.

Sometimes out of sheer exuberance they deliberately fell out of a raft, or steered into the seething waves until forced to a standstill. Some spills and at least one flip were deliberate. At times a raft might be caught in an eddy, or stuck on a smooth rock, but since everyone was laughing we recognized that it was only a caper, not a mishap. Or a raft might descend a chute sideways or even backward. It could fill with water and have to be lifted out onto flat rocks and dumped, no light chore.

No one paid any attention to two photographers on shore.

A voice would suddenly break into song, perhaps a modern lyric or more likely an old favorite, perhaps slightly risqué — such as "*Auprès de ma blonde*" sung with a leer.

They did not need drinks to raise their boisterous spirits. But drinks awaited the end of the twelve-mile float. The yellow bus met us at the takeout, and conveyed us to lunch. A number of deep metal pots heated by gas were ready to cook a fondue with thin slices of beef. Not a scrap remained as leftovers.

Back at the clubhouse, we were surprised to find that one of the photographers on shore had snapped every raft in the most exciting rapids and, it seemed, every face. He had quickly developed the color prints, and pinned them with enlargements on the bulletin board. Some were mounted and framed (good showmanship), and for a reasonable price we each could have a lasting souvenir of the day.

And that was not all. Danny Levine had taken videotapes of our antics on the river, and now we watched the playback on a large television set in the clubhouse. Danny had taken care to get everyone into the films, and our wet, happy faces laughed back at us. It was a tour de force, a remarkable ending to a high-spirited day.

The Rouge River is actually 121 miles long, and nearly all of it may be run — at the right season. The upper Rouge provides a twenty-one-mile thrill for about four weeks beginning in late April, while snowdrifts linger under the evergreens. Then the freshet subsides and the rocks show up. To reach these roadless head-waters requires a twenty-minute flight in a small aircraft, or a fifteen-minute helicopter ride from a different jumping-off place. "You plunge into many turbulent rapids," the brochure claims. "The whitewater stretches are seemingly endless, and the beauty of the river is unparalleled."

FOR FURTHER INFORMATION:

Nouveau Monde/New World River
  Expeditions Co.
5475 Paré, Suite 221
Montreal, Quebec
Canada H4P 1P7
Phone (514) 733-7166

Rivière Harricana
QUEBEC

La Rivière Harricana (emphasis on the last syllable, which adds a "w" when it crosses into Ontario) snakes and plunges for some two hundred miles north of Amos, a town on the Canadian National Railway in northern Quebec. There it meets the salty tidewater of Baie James, the very "bottom" of Hudson Bay. Swollen by tributaries, the river bulges into lakelike expansions, creates silt islands, and romps through so many rapids that you're not sure where one ends and the next begins.

The outfitters Nouveau Monde of Montreal were first to raft this river, in 1976, and Wilderness Tours of Beachburg, Ontario, followed. Each conducts two trips five or six days long per summer season, between spring freshet and late summer's diminished flow. Both outfitters rely on chartering a floatplane at the Matagami, Quebec, seaplane base. When the river level threatens to puncture his aluminum pontoons, the pilot may refuse the charter.

Thus it happened that the airplane landed our group on a convenient lake nearby. A helicopter conveyed us close to our first campsite, where flat rock made a good landing possible. There it settled on ice-scoured granite, and quickly, with a swish and roar of blades and the thumbs-up signal, the whirlybird soared away for a second load.

(Unhappily for me, the pilot let down the sling of tents and deflated rafts with a thump on the bare rock. A bottle of wine and one of shampoo took the rap. My sleeping bag reeked until aired in hot sunlight.)

Actually, the mishap became the source of a lot of good-natured badinage, for these young French-Canadians brought with them their bonhomie, their good cheer and laughter. Most were fluently bilingual, slipping from French to English and back again with ease.

All was not unalloyed delight, for the mosquitoes that hatch hungry in northern woodlands soon discovered us, and we discovered "the leetle black fly of Ontario." The voracious big moose flies were more easily avoided in a smudge or a strong wind. Most retired with nightfall, but summer nights are very short at latitude 53°N.

Two guests proved no-show, and no one knew how to contact them. As we stopped for a snack at the put-in place, however, we heard the unscheduled clatter of the helicopter once more. "What in the world . . . ?"

To reach the winding Harricana, guests ride on a floatplane and, if necessary, on a helicopter *(inset)*. Kayak and other gear also arrive via helicopter.

Raft squeezes through rocks to negotiate one of the many rapids of the Harricana.

The 'copter sat down squarely on the shore and out hopped Art, one of the missing guests. He had been in Matagami, had even viewed our group across the hotel's *salle à manger*, but was convinced that the departure was the next day. He had sauntered down to the seaplane base to inquire about the takeoff, only to learn we had already departed. A man of action, Art simply chartered the helicopter himself.

"Sure, it cost me seven hundred bucks, but it was either that or miss out on a once-in-a-lifetime trip. This'll teach me to get my dates straight!"

Art at once threw himself into helping the crew assemble the two eighteen-foot orange rafts and pump them up to three pounds pressure. They set them and two guardian kayaks afloat, for our first camp lay a few miles downstream, just above the rapids we could hear growling. A cool wind blew upriver, and we wondered whether it might be too chilly to sleep. But the sun-warmed granite under our sleeping bags made a pre-warmed mattress, while the aurora borealis danced and flickered in the dusk.

We made camp at the confluence of the small Rivière Kitci, and next morning frolicked through the whitewater of *rapides* Pawitigojic and Opwagan. The names were a reminder that this area is the hunting and trapping grounds of the Eastern Cree. For more than three centuries these Indians have paddled their canoes to the Hudson's Bay Company trading posts of Rupert's House and Moose Factory, on this and other rivers coursing down north from the Laurentian Highlands to James Bay.

Where the river widened, islands of silt showed up, their vegetation shaved off as if by a gigantic bulldozer — the work of ice jams in spring breakup. The ground would send up a thicket of willows in short order.

There are so many rapids on the Harricana as it winds through remote, lonesome country — we met not a soul on the seventy-five miles we rafted, until the last day — that any traveler is free to name them at will. The most spectacular site on the river appears to have no name on the topographical map, and thus is variously called the Big Splat and Satan's Falls. Here the river drops 30 feet of a total 750 feet between our put-in and takeout.

There are actually three narrow channels through which the river raced too violently even for our two experienced kayakers. One channel looked to be only six feet wide at the top — one could have leaped it in a running jump. I assumed we might line the rafts through the straightest channel, but instead we portaged our gear, and then the guides and kayakers lowered the empty rafts by stout nylon ropes down into calmer water. We guests made our way down to each raft, clutching the rope, finding toeholds in the rock wall. One by one the boatmen guided us into the bobbing rafts, then cast off. Our raft shot out of the final hundred yards of the gorge like a cannonball, and into high-piled foam at the foot of the rapids. The sun glinted on its iridescent bubbles, some more than two feet in diameter. Should one admire the coloration, or deplore pollution on a wilderness river?

By the time the second raft was hurled out of the chasm, the sky had darkened and a sudden wind howled like a banshee. I had set up my tent and had great difficulty keeping it from blowing away. I struggled to hold it in place from the inside, with head and arms rammed into the windward side and the rain driving in on the horizontal. The battle was waged for nearly half an hour. My fellow rafters huddled in the lee of rafts propped up by oars.

A raft waits at the foot of the gash called the Big Splat — a 30-foot drop.

Only the guides run this rapid on the Harricana, with its churning whitewater and rock outcrops.

Then, as suddenly as it began, the storm was over and everyone was laughing and chattering in nervous relief as we wrung out sodden clothing and dried blankets around a campfire.

A number of small accidents happened in the Class IV rapids next day. Our boatman's oar struck a rock, glanced off, and slashed my lip, though my helmet took the brunt of the blow. Two guests flipped overboard, and so did Pierre, the guide on the second raft. And our cook, who doubled as a guard in one of the kayaks, went overboard without a life jacket, an object lesson to the rest of us. By the time a raft could be maneuvered to where she clung to a rock, she was thoroughly chilled, though the Harricana is not considered cold.

By the fourth day we reached the lowlands, where the river serpentined through endless miles, it seemed, of muskeg and pointed spruce with the occasional stand of jack pine. We saw no wildlife except for gulls on a rocky islet, and the one moose glimpsed earlier from the helicopter. Someone went through the motions of fishing, though our guides admitted, "No one ever caught anything in this river."

Next morning, fog blanketed the river under low clouds. Remembering the discomfort of the storm, I prudently inaugurated my brand-new wetsuit, which fit like a glove over my string underwear. Encased in that, my feet snug in booties, I was warm and comfortable and dry through half a dozen big rapids.

A series of three major rapids romped below, first the Block, named for a big rock in the middle, then the Toiletbowl, of awesome velocity and turbulence. We just avoided its hole, or eddy, only to be hit broadside by solid water. The third rapid, the Drain, proved to be a lesser affair. Whichever raft took the lead, the other guests and boatman studied its progress, cheering or screaming advice or laughing when the run was successful. There was always lengthy consultation before launching into a new rapid, and invariably a post-mortem for the benefit of the second raft trip and for next year.

The second raft gained by the experience of the lead raft, and this day we landed under some jack pines for lunch. Our cook was better at kayaking than at cooking, and some guests grumbled. Obviously the catering had

little priority. By the next meal we were out of bread and coffee.

The Pretzel proved a long and difficult rapid, and certainly wet for anyone not sealed into a wetsuit. Another longish, turbulent stretch of whitewater ended with a sudden drop of about six feet, aptly named the Surprise. We were thrown to the bottom of the raft, which came up half-full of water. We bailed the water out before tackling the Rock Garden, so littered with stones and boulders that it was difficult to choose the best route.

A few ripples occurred farther down, but the river had reached flat land and we all had to paddle to keep headway. The river, fed by melting snow and rain in the hills, had become a notable stream by now. We paddled to tidewater, almost to the estuary, to find a suitable location for the floatplane to come down.

By the fifth day, the river bent westward to enter the province of Ontario and become the Harricanaw on the map.

A rock shelf, with the Harricana River on three sides, makes a unique site for a camp.

13

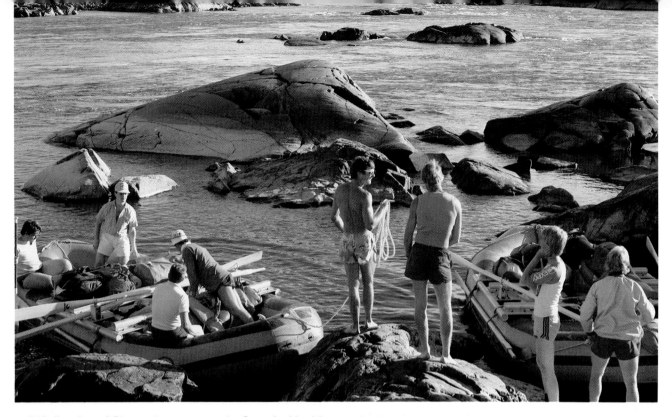

Seeing that gear is checked and heads counted, crew readies the rafts for a sunny morning on the Harricana.

FOR FURTHER INFORMATION:

Nouveau Monde/New World River Expeditions Co.
5475 Paré, Suite 221
Montreal, Quebec
Canada H4P 1P7
Phone (514) 733-7166

Wilderness Tours
Box 89
Beachburg, Ontario
Canada K0J 1C0
Phone (613) 582-3351

14

"Ah," quipped Pierre, "now we are in Canada. You'd better behave yourselves." (This was a subtle reminder of Quebec's aspirations to independence from the rest of Canada, and a sly dig at Ontario's presumed prudishness.)

On what we expected was the final day, we paddled five hours against a headwind and the incoming tide. We came upon a large, empty goose-shooting camp of numerous huts. The interior walls were scribbled with grafitti, where the brave killers boasted of being "Top Guns of the North," having bagged seventy-two geese. Other scrawls claimed higher scores.

We camped for that last night on Seven-Mile Island, shared with a colony of bank swallows and a beached gosling whose blue goose parents beat frantically up and down the river. Here we dismantled and deflated the rafts and rolled them up, ready for the pickup tomorrow. Everything was packed except our tents and bedrolls. There was no food left. Someone at headquarters had miscalculated. After all, only two trips a year do not provide much experience.

In the North a rendezvous is a sacred trust, for there is no alternative transportation, no food resource when far from any trading post, and no fish in some of the rivers. Bon mots about "living off the land" fell flat, for we had encountered nothing edible except wild onions a long way back.

It was with tremendous relief that, one day late, we heard the drone of an airplane and saw the brown water spray out from the pontoons. "Make it snappy," the pilot shouted. "It's shallow here and the tide's going out."

We hustled and were soon loaded. Then Pierre made the mistake of swatting a moose fly against the plexiglass window. The pane promptly fell out into three feet of water, and it cost some minutes to locate it and stick it back in place with tape — while the tide ran out and the pontoons settled on the bottom. All the men were in the river to their waists, pushing and heaving in the race against time and tide.

We won. The plane floated, and took off. In an hour we were back in Matagami.

Ottawa River
QUEBEC • ONTARIO

Stretching more than 700 miles, the Ottawa is the longest and strongest of the many rivers originating in the Laurentian Highlands. It rises in Quebec and threads through lakes large and small, gathering tributaries and power. This magnificent river drains some fifty thousand square miles of forest and swamp. In its upper reaches are sundry very large power dams, which create huge reservoirs of impounded water. But controls allow sufficient flow to maintain plenty of whitewater below.

From Lake Temiskaming south to Montreal, the Ottawa forms the four hundred-mile boundary between the provinces of Quebec and Ontario, with Canada's capital, Ottawa/Hull, astride the river.

La Grande Rivière du Canada became the pathway to the West for French explorers and English fur traders. It was a shortcut from the much longer route via lakes Ontario and Erie. In prehistoric times, Lake Superior drained eastward by way of the Ottawa Valley, until today's pathway of Great Lakes opened up, draining through the St. Lawrence Valley. French-Canadian voyageurs used to paddle to the beat of the chant *C'est l'aviron qui nous mène en haut* (It's the paddle that takes us up-country).

The summer flow of the Ottawa is comparable to that of the Colorado and both sustain their flow through the season. "They never turn off," rafters declare, though the Ottawa runs beneath ice for several months of winter. In contrast to most of Canada's rafting rivers, which are spawned by glaciers, the Ottawa is only refreshingly cold — in fact, relatively warm. Fed by rain and melted snow, the water courses many miles through sun-warmed ground before it reaches the best rafting section, *Rocher Fendu* (Splitrock).

Half a dozen outfitters have made this nineteen-mile segment of the Ottawa the most popular rafting in Canada. Beginning in 1975 with a mere seventy-five clients, rafters there now tally a thousand times that figure. This location is the apex of a triangle of Canada's densest population, the three big cities — Montreal, Ottawa and Toronto — to say nothing of the northeastern United States.

The Ottawa River below Ottawa City had notable rapids, now subdued by canals. Above the city, the upper river, the stretch between Lake Temiskaming and Ottawa, remains untrammeled by manmade structures. There are, though, occasional reminders of the immense log booms once anchored to the shore, the rafts of squared timber designed for the Royal Navy — rafts so huge that entire crews of rivermen lived on them for weeks as they floated down to *La Fleuve St. Laurent* (a flood too great to be called merely a river).

Each rafter on the Ottawa wears a high-buoyancy life jacket and a green helmet; some don wetsuits.

Where the Ottawa makes a great loop around *Ile de Grand Calumet* (Big Peace Pipe Island), it flows in three main channels between nearly two hundred islets, breaking in silvery foam. A twelve-mile section froths and rears up in standing waves of Class IV and V caliber. It was here that Samuel de Champlain, "the father of New France," found his canoe piling up against a rock and water gushing over the gunwale and over him.

"In this danger I cried aloud to God," and almost immediately another wave released the craft.

Today the thrills remain, but in unsinkable compartmented rafts. Grownups, like children, enjoy a scare,

secure in the knowledge that everything is as safe as life jacket and plastic helmet can make it.

Three established companies own most of the rafts in this location. Hermann Kirckhoff and his wife, Christa, both expert kayakers and canoeists, started their raft/canoe/kayak outfitting on the Madawaska, a tributary to the Ottawa, then shifted most of their activities to Foresters Falls, on the south side of the Ottawa opposite Calumet Island. They called their outfit Ottawa Whitewater Leaders, OWL for short.

Wilderness Tours of Beachburg, Ontario, pioneered rafting on the Ottawa, and with seventy rafts is the largest outfit. While on busy holiday weekends the rafters may queue up, waiting their turn to push off, the river is not over-utilized. It is a mighty river with room for all who come and many more. Wilderness Tours offers one- and two-day trips on the river and five-day trips on the Harricana in Quebec.

These and others offer daily trips, at a price of about fifty dollars a day (1987). All offer other diversions on shore — archery, volleyball, rock-climbing, wind-surfing, horseshoe-pitching, or survival games. Invariably there's a bonfire at night, and often a Saturday night dance. All now follow the safety devices pioneered by OWL. The hockey helmets are no longer considered sissy.

A third major outfitter on the *Rocher Fendu* is Ottawa Whitewater Rafting, which also operates on the Magnetawan River, Ontario, in early spring.

We reached the OWL campground at Foresters Falls, Ontario, to find it throbbing with rock'n'roll music. A group of some sixty young people had set up their tents, were celebrating the "Thank God it's Friday" syndrome with abandon, and the beer flowed. "Drink up, fellas," one shouted. "No drink on the river tomorrow, you know."

"This sort of thing doesn't happen often," Kirckhoff apologized, as we signed the usual waiver freeing the outfitter from responsibility in case of accident. But we turned tail and headed for a quiet motel.

Certainly next morning all was orderly, though it was evident some had been carousing till dawn. Most were able to join us newcomers at the hearty breakfast of French toast and maple syrup, bacon and coffee.

A twenty-minute ride up along the river in the now-familiar yellow buses brought our 190 guests to the put-in at the head of the twelve-mile stretch of fast water that we would run. Most of the guests were young and excited, a few with hangovers. Some scampered around in red-and-black wetsuits, rented at five dollars a day. We were each issued a high-buoyancy scarlet life jacket, a modified green helmet and a paddle.

Then followed the usual five-minute briefing on how to act in case of danger: falling overboard, swamping, or grounding on a rock. We were shown how to tie on our spectacles, if any. Then we in the final group were off like pebbles from a slingshot, snatched by the

Special footrest for the oarsman gives extra leverage for navigating the fast-running Ottawa.

**OWL Rafting (spring, summer,
  fall address)**
Box 29
Foresters Falls, Ontario
Canada K0J 1V0
Phone (613) 646-2054

OWL Rafting (winter address)
2 Tuna Court
Don Mills, Ontario
Canada M3A 3L1
Phone (416) 447-8845

Wilderness Tours
Box 89
Beachburg, Ontario
Canada K0J 1C0
Phone (613) 582-3351

Ottawa Whitewater Rafting Ltd.
Box 179
Beachburg, Ontario
Canada K0J 1C0
Phone (613) 646-2501

powerful current that hurled us at once into the turmoil of McCoy Chute. From the rafts ahead of ours, the leaping waves drew small screams and nervous laughter.

We shot down the rapids before we had time to evaluate what we were getting into. Then we were in flatter, more placid water.

"Paddle for that raft ahead," Greg directed with a huge grin. "Give 'em a dousing. It's all in fun, and that's what you're here for."

I got a bailing bucket of river water smack in my face. It wasn't cold — refreshing, rather — and not so very wetting since I wore bathing trunks, an old sweater and a yellow slicker as suggested. We had drawn first blood by splashing those rafters with our paddles, and they retaliated with solid water. It was all exhilarating once you entered into the spirit of things. No one got hurt, and the mock battle ended when the next rapids hove in sight. But the raft now had to be bailed out, and we used the buckets for their intended purpose. (Actually, a good percentage of any raft trip is spent in flat water. It's not all high-strung fever pitch.)

The weather was sunny and pleasant, and the dozen or so rafts on the river were well spaced out except at Garvin's Chute, the only one of three channels navigable in midsummer. The chutes comprised five sets of rapids, culminating in a last dive into the roller-coaster series of Muskrat Rapids. The peak of this series is the Coliseum, Class V rapids generated by ledges with the resulting hydraulics and long trains of standing waves, a fitting climax to whitewater adventure.

Approaching these rapids from below in 1613, Champlain and his men prudently took to the portage trail, and somewhere along the path whoever was carrying the precious astrolabe lost it. This navigational instrument for gauging the height of known stars, and thus determining one's position, was rediscovered three centuries later, when an American canoeist stumbled over it on the trail and donated it to a museum in the city of Boston.

Low overhead a helicopter dawdled, two men looking out the doors, scanning the river. We assumed they were reconnoitering the rapids and rocks, or perhaps taking official photographs. As we floated down the final

Paddles dig into whitewater as raft runs the *Rocher Fendu* (Splitrock) rapids of the Ottawa — with two men overboard.

fast water, some guests deliberately flipped overboard to bodysurf the rest of the way, paddling with their hands to the waiting restaurant-barge anchored in the quiet water at the foot of the turbulence.

The brochure had promised a gourmet lunch, and although it was not quite that, the bratwurst was very acceptable. As we ate, the barge's motor purred and we moved downriver to the OWL campground. The earlier rafters had waited lunch for us, and now we discovered the reason for the helicopter and for the grave mien of Christa Kirckhoff. Three guests in the second contingent had not only been bumped out of the raft — a frequent and usually comic event — but one had not surfaced. He was presumed to have drowned. The body was recovered two years later.

The lunchers had lost their high spirits of yesternight, and now conversed in muted tones.

The accident had happened in the furious stretch of whitewater, Garvin's Chute. Of five OWL rafts, three, steered by boatmen in bow and stern, ran the chute with no particular difficulty. The fourth, steered by only one guide in the stern, bounced off a hydraulic (a stationary wall of water thrown up beside a strong downward current or "hole" in the river) about forty feet from shore.

A guest in the raft ahead dared to look behind, and saw the young man "spinning around for a couple of minutes. Then his life jacket came off and he went under." The victim had rollicked his last, and had evidently been too befuddled this morning to tie his life jacket properly.

A young woman student with a face swollen and scratched was also involved. "When I was flung out of the raft somehow I was trapped under it. When I got free, I was floating down the river and kept blacking out. In conscious moments, I was aware that my life jacket was saving my life. I was sure glad of the safety rules."

It was ironic that the first, and to date (1987) the only, rafting fatality on the Ottawa occurred on a trip of OWL, the outfit that made such a fetish of safety.

Magnetawan River
ONTARIO

The southern edge of the Canadian Shield hangs well down into Ontario. On this fringe lies Algonquin Provincial Park, beloved of canoeists. The Magnetawan River rises in the northeastern corner of the park, straggles over smooth bedrock through a forest of mixed hardwoods and through frontier farming communities, then threads through Byng Inlet to Georgian Bay. This slender inlet gave the Ojibwa name Maganatawan (long bay) to the entire river — ten times the inlet's length.

Its turbulent water is concentrated in a nine-mile stretch, a series of ten rapids ranging in difficulty from Class II to V, the latter quite capable of tossing you out of the raft's well into the churning water. It does happen, once in a while, even to an experienced boatman. The mandatory life jacket keeps you afloat and a lineman on shore throws you a lifeline, so what appeared frightening very soon has become exciting adventure.

A raft trip of five hours is just the thing for a timid novice from Toronto, who drives due north for three and a half hours to the Magnetawan depot of the Ottawa Whitewater Rafting company. But the fact is that the Magnetawan can be run only at high water, for about

Briefing prepares guests for their Magnetawan trip.

Rafters settle themselves and their gear.

Fierce rapids on the Magnetawan entertain observers on the banks as well as paddlers.

four weeks starting in mid-April. After high water, the rafts are deflated and trucked back to Beachburg, to serve on the *Rocher Fendu*.

The actual rafting begins at Knoefli (pronounced nuffly) Falls Bridge. Our eight rafts, fully inflated, bobbed in the fast water, waiting for our group to arrive by bus. "Usually a party consists of eighty percent first-timers," Sean, our head guide, told me. "Some fifteen percent have already shot the Ottawa rapids with our company. Perhaps five percent are simply rafting nuts who will join any group on any river."

We were issued the usual scarlet life jackets, and yellow helmets over black wetsuits. To the curious crowd hanging over the bridge railings, each raft must have looked like a floating flower bed.

Each of the eight black neoprene rafts was composed of four cross-tubes in which we sat comfortably, as in a bus.

21

The second rapid below the bridge is a major chute, the tricky Poverty Bay Rapids. Here all the rafts tied up to shore while the guides studied the hydraulics of two turbulent drops named the Toaster and Kellogg's Drop.

Water levels change from day to day in spring, and thus the currents as well. So the guides lined themselves up along shore at the danger points, armed with throw-lines, and the lead raft maneuvered into position. We picked up an extra crewman to paddle in the bow, and each of us was ready with a paddle.

From the stern, Sean shouted, "Paddle!"

We dug in. Once the raft is drawn into the flow, there's no changing your mind, getting off, or even stopping. You're committed.

We slid into the boiling waters, paddling madly so Sean could control our raft with his long oars as we plunged through the narrow, twisting drops. We were tossed like chips, spray engulfed us, and solid water crashed in. I noticed the white knuckles of the girl who sat next to me. Then, suddenly, we were through.

Laughing and gasping, we leaned toward the next assault a few yards ahead. The run took only a minute or so, but we all felt the surge of adrenalin, and the sense of triumph as we drifted leisurely ashore in a backwater. There we shook off the river and bailed the raft, while Sean ran back upstream along the bank to help pilot the next raft through.

In the following raft, one passenger was bounced high and out. "When I came down," he recounted later, "the raft had gone ahead, and there I was in the drink." He floated high in the extra-buoyant life jacket, perfectly dry and warm in his wetsuit. He easily grabbed the lifeline thrown to him and was quickly pulled ashore. We spectators raised a cheer.

"It was the greatest!" he exclaimed with a guffaw.

As our raft breasted the waves of another rapid, our guide in the stern suddenly found himself rowing the air while the raft buckled and reared up. He quickly recovered his balance and his poise.

Rafts follow each other along quiet water, the home stretch on the Magnetawan.

The rapids of the Magnetawan during April and May are to be respected, rated by experts as Class IV/V — in layman's language "heavy but runnable."

Later in the day we floated on rippling water through beautiful roadless country, through forests of poplar, spruce and birch, where white trilliums starred the open glades. Then came Sellars' Canyon.

"This is a technical chute," Sean told us, "and I must first carefully study the currents and spots to avoid, and discuss them with my colleagues."

The brochure speaks of hairpin turns . . . white-knuckle wheelies . . . dinosaur-sized hydraulics. It all seemed rather dramatic. Still, when Sean steered us out of a back eddy once again and into Ross Rapids, it didn't seem much overstated. In an "over-'n-out" wave, our raft got hung up on a submerged rock and swung broadside to the falls, with water pouring over the gunwale. Rocking our weight from side to side, paddling and pushing did no good. When it was obvious we couldn't get loose, a crewman on shore threw us a line and we pulled away, Sean's ears red from the good-natured joshing.

After that small adventure the rest was uneventful. Helping the diminished current, we paddled to the takeout — the end of the Bullet's trajectory. Since this was the last run of the 1984 season, we helped the guides pull all the rafts from the water. Once deflated, they would be rolled up and loaded on a truck for transfer back to the Ottawa River, where the rapids "never stop running."

FOR FURTHER INFORMATION:

Ottawa Whitewater Rafting Ltd.
P.O. Box 179
Beachburg, Ontario
Canada K0J 1C0
Phone (613) 646-2501

Pigeon River
MANITOBA

Most visitors to Manitoba get the impression of quiet, well-behaved rivers serpentining through muddy prairie, rivers like the Assiniboine and the Red, or the Saskatchewan.

But to the east, where the Canadian Shield shoulders into the plains, other rivers foam and froth their winding way through and over smooth, glaciated Precambrian granite.

Three "wild" rivers (the Pigeon, the Berens and the Poplar), untrammeled by man's bridges or dams, cascade into the eastern shore of Lake Winnipeg north of the Narrows. All three of these rivers knew fleets of birchbark canoes bringing furs to the trading post at Berens River. The names of both hamlet and river commemorate Joseph Berens, a long-gone governor of the Hudson's Bay Company.

Veteran outfitter Jack Clarkson of Berens River has rafted all three streams and made them accessible. He combines river rafting with his hunting and fishing business, and knows the watershed like the back of his hand, both from canoe level and from the cockpit of his wheeled Cessna.

All three rivers have their share of rapids and chutes, but the Berens is the most formidable and therefore most exciting. However, a four-day raft trip on the Pigeon best suited my personal timetable.

It is a one-hour hop from Winnipeg International Airfield by Perimeter Airways scheduled flight. We landed on a dirt strip at Berens River just as a Beaver floatplane landed on the water.

Its Cree pilot, Don Baxter, disembarked with two guests whom he had picked up by arrangement at Jackhead Point, fifteen minutes' flying time across Lake Winnipeg. They had motored some 156 miles north of Winnipeg; Berens River village cannot be reached by road.

We were each issued a large waterproof bag to hold our personal gear. While we snacked and got acquainted, Jack, the pilot Don, and our boatmen, Jeff and Ray, flew off in the Beaver to set up camp far up the Pigeon River. We would float down more than 85 miles.

When we guests arrived the tents were set up neatly — thereafter we would set up our own — and the guides were busy assembling our sixteen-foot green raft.

Jack departed with the Beaver, and Jeff started the campfire. Is there anything more mouthwatering than a good steak sizzling on the embers of a wood fire? Well, perhaps coffee and bacon announcing to your nose after a windy, thundery night that breakfast is about ready.

Anyone who thinks Manitoba cannot offer exciting whitewater rafting should have been with us. With the

Boatman Jeff Rennicke *(above)* brought his skills from the Colorado to the Pigeon. A guest *(facing page)* snaps a shot of a raft in the rapids.

Time for fishing — for walleye and pike — is part of a Pigeon River trip.

help of a small outboard motor we skimmed over calm reaches of dark brown water, moving slowly, scarcely bending the stems of water weeds. Then the stems would wave as the current quickened, and Jeff would take to the long oars.

In no time, we approached tumultous rapids and chutes that would awe anyone, even those accustomed to the swift rivers of the Rockies.

The Pigeon's many rapids are not to be despised; wild, boiling waters plunge among polished rocks. To be navigated successfully they require all the skill of an experienced boatman. Jeff Rennicke, for all his rafting on other rivers, was a newcomer to the Pigeon, and prudently took time to reconnoiter dangerous falls and obstacles to locate the safest routes through the leaping waves.

Once the drop was so steep that it was necessary to line the raft through fast water and over the rocks — a precaution used by the fur brigades. Jeff held the stern rope, Ray the bow, and we guests carried our most precious belongings and trudged over the slippery rock. That was the only "portage" we made.

More than once I looked down into a deep hole formed in a whirlpool, but it was behind us before anyone had time to take alarm.

There were splendid camping sites, we noted as we hurtled past. Rafts, however, travel with the current and cannot backtrack. The result was a couple of dismal campgrounds in a lovely landscape.

Having rafted on other Canadian rivers, I was surprised again and again by such beauty in central Manitoba, a wilderness of forest and streams and wildlife. Two black bears reared up for a better look at this strange object floating by. We spied a mink slipping over the rocks at the water's edge, and the big brown head of a cow moose swimming across Round Lake near the fire watchtower.

We moved even more quietly than in a canoe, and could surprise a great blue heron spearing frogs in the shallows, then flapping up into the air on wide wings.

I remember so well the mist rising from the water's surface in early morning, and how the far shore seemed, by mirage, to be lifted in air. Evening brought the song of the vesper sparrow and of the hermit thrush, all in a fragrant aroma of wild mint.

In early evening some of the others wetted a fishing line for walleye and pike. One of the pike was so large that a young fisherman broke his rod attempting to land it without a net.

As the campfire burned down, Jeff recalled for us incidents from his rafting on the Colorado and the rivers of Idaho. He admitted, "My heart is not in those mountains! It's living on a northern river where the loons call at night, like here. So I'll be back on some sort of hiking and river trips next year."

Thus for four peaceful days we drifted downstream, meeting not a soul. By arrangement, our Indian pilot picked us up near the outlet of the Pigeon, above its final cascade, and whisked us back to Berens River. There Jack took over and flew us out to Winnipeg — quite a culture shock after the silence and serenity of a little-known aspect of Manitoba.

I, too, will be back for more, tempted by those larger, riskier waves on the Berens River.

A sloping rock is a fine place to dry out wet gear, organize provisions, and relax.

FOR FURTHER INFORMATION

**North Country River Trips
Berens River, Manitoba
Canada R0B 0A0
Phone (204) 382-2284
(204) 382-2379**

The Prairies

Between the Canadian Shield and the Rocky Mountains unrolls the vast northern extension of the Great American Plain. Early French explorers emerging from a thousand miles of evergreen forest discovered the treeless plains and exclaimed, *"La prairie!"* (meadowland). English Henry Kelsey, trending westward from the muddy Hudson Bay Lowlands, noted, "The ground begins for to be more bared than it used to."

Only with the passing of years and exploration from the north was it learned that the flat land reached from the Gulf of Mexico to the Arctic Ocean. The land had sunk under four ice ages. As the first ice melted it left behind a vast swamp where dinosaurs lumbered and fought, and left their bones in the sediment. In the last ice age, hairy mammoths roamed and left their bones in ice.

The legacy of that vast prehistoric inland sea is an infinitude of sloughs, ponds, lakes and streams of all sizes. Because the terrain is relatively level there is comparatively little whitewater, though many a ripple and the occasional waterfall. Many rapids have been drowned for electricity. The result is little whitewater rafting in the central prairie.

On the northern border of the prairie province of Alberta, the Slave River drains northward, its sixteen miles of fierce rapids of Class V quality.

From its start high in the Canadian Rockies, the Oldman River wanders across Alberta, a prairie province.

Oldman River

ALBERTA

The prairies are bounded on the west by the Rockies. But first come the foothills, their spines draped with forest pelts in the form of national and provincial and wilderness parks.

Most southerly of the three foothill rivers that I rafted with a commercial outfit is the Oldman, which rises on the slope of Mount Tornado to flow eastward and join the famous Bow, which races through Banff. Together they join the Red Deer and become the South Saskatchewan, which serpentines through the rich prairie wheatlands into the province of Manitoba.

The springtime freshet does not last long in any of these mountain rivers, and it comes early, with the melt of a sunny day hardening into ice in a cool night.

I joined a group of a dozen on June 2, and found the Oldman River water glacially cold. I was grateful for the warmth of a rented wetsuit; sweater, heavy socks and booties I carried with me. The river ran gray-green with glacial silt foaming over and around boulders. From Crowsnest Pass we had reached the Oldman River Recreation Area by branching off the Kananaskis Forest Reserve Road, and would "do" the river in two stages. The Oldman was first run commercially in 1979, the lower and easier run first, then as now. The river is seldom more than thirty yards wide, and remarkably even.

The morning run took about two hours of floating quickly over the clean river, every rock showing through the limpid water. At noon we and our two rafts were picked up and returned to the campsite for a

Rafts race (above) through a turbulent stretch on the Oldman, and negotiate (right) an obstruction — a natural rock ledge.

30

snack. The air was full of the winey fragrance of opening poplar buds.

Then came the upper segment, taking a similar length of time but giving a more difficult ride. A longish, twisting canyon rose over many rocks. There was even snow in shaded corners, and all along, wild ducks took to the air as we approached. A couple of eagles cruised above and a white mountain goat stood stiffly, watching us out of slanted yellow eyes. After a couple of hours we stopped at a low bank, hastily overturned our rafts to drain, then lugged them up the bank to the waiting vehicles. This early in the season, neither mosquito nor fly was abroad at this altitude.

The Oldman was plenty of fast-water ripples, really about Class II difficulty. Even so, a man in the second raft was bounced out, but quickly retrieved.

We were as hungry as he at dinner time, and the appetizing aroma of barbecued steaks compensated for a certain ache in muscles out of practice in paddling energetically in fast water.

Our young cook, well experienced in outdoor cookery, served stir-fried vegetables. He topped an excellent meal with a dessert new to me — bananas browned in Kahlua and butter, rolled in crushed walnuts and coconut, wrapped in foil and served hot — delectable! We sat on segments of log at tables provided by the Forestry Service of Alberta.

The sawed-off logs became fireside seats at the campfire, where the young people fell into noisy, happy conversation. I looked at the waxing moon, and the gurgling Oldman crooned me to sleep in no time.

I had hung my mesh underwear on my tent pole to drip dry. It froze stiff during the night, but I was warm inside tent and sleeping bag. The mesh soon dried on my body as I sat near the cookfire and forked down a hearty breakfast of pancakes, syrup, sausages and peach halves. We all ate with an appetite, and swilled down quantities of camp coffee before going on to our next rafting adventure on the Highwood River.

Sliced potatoes head for the frying pan as the cook prepares a tasty meal over the campfire.

FOR FURTHER INFORMATION:

Alberta Adventure Guide
Travel Alberta
Government of Alberta
Box 2500
Edmonton, Alberta
Canada T5J 2Z4
Phone (800) 222-6501

8

Highwood River
ALBERTA

This river is often run in conjunction with the Oldman, giving a day to each on a single weekend. The Highwood rises in Banff National Park, Alberta, races down the eastern slope of the Rockies, through the town of High River, then streaks north to join the chill green Bow River southeast of Calgary. It swirls and ripples all its young life, to the delight of rafters.

The rafting here is confined to the month of June, and to a fourteen-mile segment where the river drops 650 feet. It is a tricky river, with rapids classed III and IV.

About forty guests had already assembled for the day's run when we arrived, and five rafts were already inflated. A dozen trailers and campers were parked there, for the river's fast water suits the trout and thus the sport fishermen.

Though the river riots downhill, we had to paddle almost continuously — not to make headway, but to avoid rocks. It is nearly all rapids and rocks as the river breaks through the mountain barrier, providing an exciting run through some narrow, twisting canyons. The stream was scarcely fifty yards wide, and very even — and just above freezing.

Fishermen perched on the banks and cast their nearly invisible nylon lines out over the sparkling water. Their dog companions paced the banks, unsure whether or not to bark at this strange flotilla of dark

Paddles are distributed before rafters set out on the Highwood.

33

Watchful raft crew *(left)* runs whitewater on the Highwood while photographer captures the scene.

A young rafter *(above)* smiles though she's been drenched. The Highwood has shallows *(above right)* where guests must walk a little.

gray monsters slipping silently past, paddles a-drip. The fishermen must have hated us because, as we swept around the many curves, we could not know their lines were waiting to entangle us.

Two passengers were flipped overboard, but since everyone wore wetsuits no one suffered from the cold water. In fact, water fights broke out with the greatest of good humor. One raft lying in wait or passing close to another would be showered with a bailing bucket of river water, or be splashed with paddles. It really turned into a wet, hilarious combat, involving sleek maidens and brawny youths. Such ebullience was thus proved not Franco-Canadian only.

Our pretty cook had arrived by bus and had laid out the lunch "makin's" on the short turf at the top of a sixty-foot cutbank above our haul-out, where we drew the raft well up out of reach of the tugging current.

Two long ropes dangled from stout trees on top, and these were our means of ascent. Hanging onto a rope, we climbed up hand over hand, bracing our feet against the clay bank. Up, up, we climbed and every one of us made it successfully. We assembled sandwiches to our liking, washed them down with flavorful coffee, and pondered second helpings.

Three mature guests decided they had had enough bouncing down the Highwood (or preferred to avoid the rope descent). They walked back to our waiting bus.

The rest of us voted for a second helping of rafting, and swarmed down the bank for more splashing and another couple of hours. It was all fun and refreshing, and it felt good, too, when the buses came for us. We got into dry clothing — women in the buses, men in the bushes. I'm sure all slept soundly that night.

FOR FURTHER INFORMATION:

Alberta Adventure Guide
Travel Alberta
Government of Alberta
Box 2500
Edmonton, Alberta
Canada T5J 2Z4
Phone (800) 222-6501

9

Red Deer River

ALBERTA

The Red Deer River is the most popular of the rafting rivers that course down the eastern slopes of Canada's Rocky Mountain range. It, like the Oldman and the Highwood, rises in the Continental Divide in Banff National Park, and rushes eastward with youthful ebullience to carve a giant "S" across the province of Alberta.

It begins in evergreen forest of spruce and lodgepole pine and slows through the city of Red Deer, midway between populous Edmonton and Calgary. It winds

For these rafters, quiet water on the upper Red Deer serves as a put-in place.

through prime wheatland, cutting a trough, deeper year by year, through the brown clay, so people on the flats above may be unaware of the river far below. For nearly two hundred miles the Red Deer winds through semi-arid ranch country and the badlands of stratified clay hills thick with fossils of the ancient sea and with dinosaur bones. A most dramatic section, the Dinosaur Provincial Park, has been declared a UNESCO World Heritage Property.

Some years ago my wife and I canoed down this river from Sundre in the foothills to the Saskatchewan border, a distance of roughly 400 of a total of 460 miles. The lower section has a few riffles, but is too slow for rafting thrills. We did not attempt the wilder upper reaches, having been warned that the river was too dangerous for canoes, especially in freshet.

That was before rafting became possible. A raft or a kayak can travel in complete safety where a canoe would be overwhelmed.

Roland Jonas of Wilderness Encounters, Edmonton, pioneered rafting on the upper reaches of the Red Deer, as he did on the Highwood and the Oldman, farther south, and on the Slave, farther north. All have since been taken over by other outfitters.

The brochure claimed, "The Red Deer flows through scenic alpine meadows and steep forested gorges. It

Edmonton-based Yvan Sabourin guides a raft down the Red Deer; guests do the paddling.

combines serene jade-colored pools and forty sets of whitewater rapids.''

As one proof of the dependability of his rafts, Jonas annually gave an afternoon's free pleasure, in calmer waters, to wheelchair individuals and also to the mentally retarded. On the other hand, the upper reaches have become challenging sites for kayak competitions.

Jonas ran one- and two-day trips and also half-days.

I met a handful of fellow-rafters in Sundre (much grown from the hamlet I remembered), and we piled ourselves and our gear into a van. It was a small midweek group, mostly from Calgary, warm and friendly as Westerners can be. Don drove us about fifty miles into the foothills.

We seated ourselves in the raft, perched on the high sides and clung to the hand lines. Our boatman, Yvan, though only nineteen, had spent a third of his life rafting whitewater. He sat in the stern and steered with a pair of sweeps. This being an oar-and-paddle trip, all of us paddled according to his shouted instructions.

With only a light load, our raft bounced down one rapid after another, taking spray and occasionally solid water over the blunt bow. It was great fun, and we all felt inordinately pleased with ourselves when, having approached a ledge correctly, Yvan shouted, "Good!"

A gaggle of wild ducklings skittered away at our approach to our lunch stop. Don had driven back downstream to meet us at this regular stop and had lunch laid out.

Paddles flailing *(left)*, rafters plunge down the clear waters of the Red Deer. On a more tranquil stretch of river, two guests *(above)* sit in the front of a raft.

In the afternoon we encountered rougher water, and one Calgarian was flipped overboard. Twice I was hurled into the well of the raft, as were others, but we quickly regained our seats on the sides.

Four light-hearted young fellows in wetsuits caught up and passed us in the fast water. It didn't matter to them whether they rode forward, backward or sideways down the rapids. They reminded me of the vivacious Canadiens of the Rouge River in Quebec. The last we saw of them as they were swept around a bend was some energetic bailing.

Bailing wasn't necessary for a group of kayakers having fun in the whitewater section used for competitions.

Part of the day's outing was a circle drive of some seventy miles through the vast empty parkland of Ya-ha-tinda Ranch, where an antlered mule deer frowned at our passing. A short walk brought us to a canyon where the impressive Big Horn Falls dropped in silvery splendor.

Back at our overnight campsite, we each put up our tent while Don and Yvan built a fire and cooked dinner to the purl of a small rapid.

Fallen pine needles made a soft mattress. And then it was morning, and we ran the final rapid, a good fast run over a double ledge. We pulled out at Hole Camp Ledge, close to a paved road, only ten miles west of Sundre.

FOR FURTHER INFORMATION:

Alberta Adventure Guide
Travel Alberta
Government of Alberta
Box 2500
Edmonton, Alberta
Canada T0L 0W0
Phone (800) 222-6501

The Far North

High up in the north of the central plain the rivers drain toward the Arctic Ocean, sometimes directly, as does the Coppermine; sometimes indirectly, as does the Slave, which feeds the mighty Mackenzie. While the plain is largely flat, it holds intrusions of rock and is bracketed by low mountains. Rivers that move sluggishly on the whole break into whitewater over ledges. The Nahanni turns its back on the Arctic, to flow south and enter the Mackenzie via the Liard. Instead of winding through the tundra, it cuts through ranges of solid limestone.

Out of the plain, but in the extreme north of British Columbia, the Tatshenshini carved its way through the Coast Range to reach the Pacific. The most northerly of the rivers I have rafted is the Firth, up in the peak of Yukon Territory, which flows into the Beaufort Sea, a part of the Arctic Ocean.

A remote spectacle of Canada's far north, the Nahanni's Virginia Falls plummet 316 feet.

Slave River
NORTHWEST TERRITORIES

On Alberta's northern border, the deep black gumbo of the prairies and the fringe of parkland begin to change. They merge into a final fling of the Canadian Shield, a strong forerunner of the ice-scraped bedrock of the Far North.

Stand on the high clay cutbank at Fort Smith, in the Northwest Territories, and watch the tawny waters of the Slave River leap and thunder as twice the volume of Niagara Falls rushes down north in the Rapids of the Drowned.

The River of the Slavey Indians takes its name from a scornful epithet (coward) flung at the dispossessed Beaver Indians when the encroaching Crees pushed them out from Lake Athabasca's shores. "It was by no means the idea of servitude," Alexander Mackenzie wrote in his journal in 1789, "but a term of reproach that denoted more than average savageness." Denigration of victims was even then a prime weapon in psychological warfare.

A continuous navigable waterway of 1,700 miles unrolls from Fort McMurray, on the Athabasca River in northern Alberta, all the way to the Arctic Ocean, unimpeded except for a 16-mile stretch of rapids. The Slave River, daughter of the Peace and the Athabasca rivers, flows smoothly most of its 200-mile length, but drops 125 feet here where the river hurls its silty waves over gneissic ledges in four dramatic cascades — Cassette, Pelican, Mountain, and Rapids of the Drowned — discharging 8,500 cubic yards per second.

The rapids were well-known to local Crees and Chipewyans. They guided Mackenzie into the great river that started west (he hoped to reach the Pacific), but suddenly turned north to the polar sea. He called his discovery the River of Disappointment. Other explorer/ fur-traders learned the characteristics of the Slave in their thrust northward and westward.

One such party, looking for potential trading sites, paused above the fourth and last cataract. A scouting party went on ahead, leaving five men waiting for a signal that a way had been found through the rapids. Suddenly the waiting men heard a signal, a single shot, and promptly embarked in their canoe only to be swamped in house-high standing waves. They never knew that an excitable scout had taken a potshot at a duck.

The Rapids of the Drowned is their memorial.

Nowadays, new highways and a railway bypass the rapids and also Fort Smith, long the administrative center for Canada's Northwest Territories. But a new breed of men and women tackles the rapids in eighteen-foot inflatable neoprene rafts. Still, they too avoid the curlback waves and standing waves that reach up to

forty feet and are locally called haystacks. They follow the voyageurs' route, taking the channels on the east side where hundreds of spruce-covered islands brake the river's speed. (Only a foolhardy kayaker would dare to run the cascades and falls of the Slave, but like the canoemen of old, today's rafters find the flanking channels plenty fast and challenging.)

Ingenious and energetic Roland Jonas of Edmonton, Alberta had rafted on many rivers from the Yukon to Mexico, but never on more tumultuous waters. For that very reason he inaugurated rafting on the rapids of the Slave, where the river crosses the border from Alberta to the Northwest Territories. He worked out a schedule of raft trips of varying duration from five hours to five days. A local outfitter, Dutch-born Jacques van Pelt, has added this enterprise to his SubArctic Wilderness

Adventures. Jacques is a keen naturalist, and radiates enthusiasm for life in subarctic Canada.

"This is a very special place to us."

Our leisurely three-day trip in July consisted of fourteen guests and four boatmen, including Roland Jonas in a small scarlet scout raft with an outboard motor that could, slowly, tow our three eight-by-eighteen-foot gray rafts. The rafts were already pumped up when we reached the put-in place at Fort Fitzgerald, Alberta, south of the Cassette Rapids. We were given large orange waterproof bags to hold camping and personal gear. Our cameras were sealed in handy army surplus ammunition canisters. We each donned the mandatory red life jacket, and some people rented yellow slickers.

The river is deceptively placid above Cassette, the first cascade, so one could be lulled into thinking the

Quick drop *(above left)* takes raft through a very narrow side-channel of the Slave; outstretched oars barely clear the rocks. Narrowest spots *(above)* become natural water slides.

43

Guests *(top)* put up tents on a sandy ledge by the Slave. Lunch makings *(above)* are spread on flat, sun-warmed rocks.

whole thing had been overstated. Roland explained the name. It seems that once some Hudson's Bay Company voyageurs, paddling downstream, overturned, and to the bottom went a small case (cassette) containing records of the past year and the payroll. Thereafter the Honorable Company dictated that these rapids must be portaged, not paddled.

Roland's small red raft skittered off in advance of our heavier rafts, leading the way into a narrow channel, the first of many that flanked the east side of the river, where the banks were low. The river raced through these passages unimpeded, passages often so narrow we expected to scrape on either side, and there was no room for the long oars to maneuver.

On a lakelike expansion among islands of bare bedrock, we found a sandspit on which to pitch our tents. Then, whoops! one of the narrow channels became a natural water-slide. Bathing suits topped by life jackets, one after another we leaped into the fast water.

Our feet shot out from under us and, lying back, we hurtled down the passage until cast up on shore one hundred yards beyond, often out of sight but always bobbing up again. Our young people seemed inexhaustible, running up the bare rocks and floating down so swiftly that I was reminded of a pack of lemmings. They were so absorbed that only repeated calls from our oarsmen-turned-chefs got them out.

"Come an' get it!" the cooks shouted in exasperation, "Or we'll throw it out."

The food was extraordinarily good and lavish — eight-dollar steaks, one or more per person; fresh salad; wines flowing freely; and delectable cakes baked in a Dutch oven under charcoal briquets.

Roland used his small raft for scouting channels ahead of our larger craft, because water levels varied with the season and the precipitation. Usually the channels were free of obstructions such as boulders or windfallen trees, but full of turbulent waves. We cameramen frequently were able to get off above a fast-water channel, find a good place for photographing the rafts as they bounced through, then re-board below. We never had to plead, "Just let me get one more shot," for the rafts were spaced out for our benefit.

Where the river widened to nearly two miles, the oarsmen had to bend to their long sweeps — the wind created a small chop. In spite of all the speed of the current, in places Roland had to devise a tactic to help us. He had the three rafts tied abreast, with a single line to his motorized raft, and in no time we were gliding like a raft of ducklings to the edge of Pelican Rapids.

The Pelican Rapids is really a waterfall leaping over and between islets of pink granite, polished to a high gloss through centuries of scouring waves. All around was the roar of churning, galloping water, which formed a moat around the islands where the big white pelicans have their nests. This is North America's most northerly pelican rookery, existing because the islets are safe from marauders. The swirling water protects the ungainly young from predators.

That was a memorable evening. The "Merry Dancers," as some early explorers called the Northern Lights, arabesqued across the sky.

From downriver one could have heard the rumble of the Mountain Rapids, the biggest drop of them all, were it not for the noise immediately around us of rushing water. Mountain Rapids is the most spectacular of the four sets. There is no mountain in this flat country, or even a high hill, but the name has stuck. We could see spray shooting high from a twenty-foot ledge. Again the boatmen lined the rafts over an obstruction, and we portaged our gear to a wide beach of sand below.

We sat long around the campfire this final night, after a dinner of shish kebab washed down with a lovely California wine, Pinot Noir '78.

Next noon, to celebrate our successful passage, Roland prepared a Mexican lunch that brought the young people on the run from sporting in a swift chute of water. He deftly rolled the rims of our drinking glasses in salt to make margaritas. A finely ground meat filling was heated to stuff the tacos.

Downstream roared the Rapids of the Drowned, and on the 135-foot western cutbank we could see Fort Smith's tallest buildings. We did not challenge the haystacks of the terrible rapids, but prudently slipped along the side channels and crossed the Slave below

Anne van Pelt carves a piece of diamond willow found on the Slave.

45

An empty raft, still inflated, is moved across smooth rock to avoid a sharp drop in the Slave.

the churning water. Three abreast, with Roland's small motorized raft towing us, we met Jacques van Pelt on the left bank.

Our junket ended with a conducted tour into Wood Buffalo National Park, where we did a "buffalo crouch," hunching low and slipping from tree to tree to get within ten or twelve yards of the great animals as they grazed or took dust baths.

Only park employees are allowed in the section of park where the shrinking flock of whooping cranes comes to nest each year. It was enough to see one of the immense birds flap across the sky.

The big white birds still dive for fish as they did in the voyageurs' day, bringing up a whitefish in the pouched beak, then paddling off to ingest it. To observe the deliberate, dignified, heavy wingbeats in flight is to forget how ridiculous the birds look on land.

"The breeding population is only thirty or forty pairs," Jacques van Pelt had informed us. He keeps unofficial tabs on the birds. "Around 1900, the records indicate there were usually about eighty pairs here. Still, there was an exceptionally good hatch this spring. And these birds have been declared a protected species. Aircraft must not fly lower than 2,000 feet above their nests."

Our boatmen lined the rafts through the edge of the cascade, guiding them with ropes on shore, and slid them over smooth rock. We passengers carried what we could. It was not a long portage and we took to the

Three abreast, rafts are towed back to Fort Smith takeout below the Rapids of the Drowned.

water again perilously close to a tall standing wave, ready to engulf us if we strayed into it through carelessness.

A railway to the south shore of Great Slave Lake, and a paved highway to Yellowknife on the north shore, have combined to sideline Fort Smith. The brown water still explodes on ledges, still builds up its terrifying, deadly waves.

It may not be for long. Energy-hungry Alberta has plans to build a huge dam across the Slave, costing six to eight billion dollars, and originally hoped to have it in production by 1991. A feasibility study indicates that in full production the barrier of water will supply one-third of the province's output — between 8.5 and 9.7 million kilowatt hours annually.

Against those alluring figures any argument seems puny. Shall 1.5 million horsepower be allowed to "go to waste" for the sake of a bunch of midsummer raft enthusiasts? Or for a rookery of birds? Too bad the pelicans will lose their safe islands and perish. Too bad the Indians will find their fishing and hunting in jeopardy when the resulting backup creates lakes in Wood Buffalo National Park. Sad that the world's only nesting grounds of the whooping crane will be threatened and the young birds jeopardized by hydroelectric wires. Hard cheese if the bison get foot rot in soggy pastures and are forced to find higher ground. Where will they find it?

FOR FURTHER INFORMATION:

**SubArctic Wilderness Adventures
Box 685
Fort Smith, Northwest Territories
Canada X0E 0P0
Phone (403) 872-2467**

11

Coppermine River
NORTHWEST TERRITORIES

Well within the Northwest Territories, east of Great Bear Lake, the Coppermine River rises in small Lac de Gras to straggle across the flat Barren Lands. It threads Point Lake, gathering seepage and creeks and ponds until it becomes a fair-sized stream and cuts a trench for itself in the tundra. It finally becomes a large river, finding faults in the volcanic rock and creating a torrent. After 470 miles it reaches salt water, the Arctic Ocean.

It is all a long, long way from southern Ontario, but this is the river the Remmlers chose to raft when, in 1978, they formed Arctic Waterways.

The first day of school summer vacation, Ingmar and Barbara Remmler of Stevensville load up car and van to drive more than three thousand miles to Yellowknife, capital of Northwest Territories. Their two vehicles are loaded with deflated rafts, oars, tents, and waterproof seabags — in short, all the gear needed for two weeks' rafting by five people in each of two rafts.

It's a long haul to their destination, but they usually manage it in five days of hard driving. Yellowknife, the gold-mining city on the north shore of Great Slave Lake, is headquarters for four trips a summer.

Logistics, of course, go into effect long before the departure date.

Bearded Ingmar takes evenings and weekends from his job in physics to round up fruits and vegetables and poultry in their prime, to freeze-dry them in small, neat packages for speed in preparing succulent camp meals — and to save on air freight. He buys fresh meat in Edmonton.

Yellowknife is just the jumping-off place for the rafting. The actual put-in place is northeast, 2¼ hours' flying by floatplane to land on the Coppermine above the Arctic Circle.

The river is well-known in explorers' journals, and famous in canoeing annals. Arctic Waterways rafts only 140 miles of the river's total.

Guests leave a chartered twin-engine Otter on the Coppermine.

The river foams over boulders and through gorges, dropping 970 feet to the sea. It is a great river for expert canoeists lured by wide skies and a landscape uncluttered by trees. It is not everybody's dish, which is okay since the fragile Arctic ecology does not recover quickly from invasion.

The Remmlers, an energetic outdoor couple, parents of grown children, had adventured in canoes and kayaks before being bitten with Arctic fever. In 1978 they organized Arctic Waterways, which makes four rafting trips per summer down the Coppermine to the salt water of Coronation Gulf.

All the 1983 trips were fully booked, and only by a late cancellation was I lucky enough to be included.

We landed on a calm stretch of the river below steep banks holed with the tunnels of nesting swallows, and

Forbidding, rocky cliffs mark the approach to Rocky Defile Rapids *(above)* on the Coppermine. Even in August *(below)*, a small tributary to this Far North river is iced over.

Discoveries along the Coppermine include *(clockwise from top left)* nests of cliff swallows on rocky ledges, wild onions in blossom, an abandoned trapper's camp, and a small piece of native copper.

helped carry the loads to the top, where we set up the tents. The boatmen assembled the rafts at the water's edge, and our ardent fishermen unlimbered their rods. The fast water swirling around rocks provides ideal conditions for Arctic char, grayling and the occasional trout. Before long, Oscar, the young German, was releasing fish. He just liked catching them, and took over one hundred fish on the trip. His prize catch was a ten-pound Arctic char, and we all appreciated this delectable red salmon of the Far North.

But the Coppermine took its toll. One Ontario schoolteacher quipped that the name should be changed to "the river of lost lures" when a Boston guest mourned that the river had gulped down about one hundred dollars' worth of his tackle.

The Coppermine was first tagged "the faraway metal river" by northern Indians trading at Churchill on Hudson Bay. They touted the wealth of native copper lying about, and showed the yellow knives they had hammered from it.

A fur-trade apprentice, Samuel Hearne, was sent to discover this mine of copper in 1771. After a thousand

Steaks sizzle over the campfire *(above left)* as guide
Charlie Third prepares dinner. A German guest *(above)*
pulled many Arctic char from the Coppermine.

weary miles of foot-slogging across the Barren Lands,
Hearne wrote with tempered reproach, "Their accounts
differed from the truth." Some copper still lies near the
confluence of the Kendall River. I lit upon a couple of
pieces about the size of a dime, far different from the
four-pound chunk that Hearne found.

We made an excursion across the tundra to view
some *auf* ice, old, hard glacial ice that never melted
from year to year. As usual, a small group of caribou
had sought refuge there to escape flies.

"We always see caribou here," our boatman, Charlie,
commented.

"I want to see a musk ox," demanded a fellow from
Boston, but when it was explained that the musk oxen

range far to the east and on the Arctic islands, he was
content with sighting two moose.

The most dramatic stretch of the river is a jagged slot
in the red sandstone, nearly a mile long, named Rocky
Defile by Lieut. John Franklin on his disastrous journey
of 1821. (Our rafts sailed through like the eider ducks
we observed. Franklin's voyageurs piled up on a rock
and nearly swamped.)

All equipment *(above left)* is portaged around Bloody Falls. With rafts on the shore *(above)*, fisherman tries for Arctic char at the foot of the falls.

Rocky Defile has claimed more than its share of lives. Half a dozen canoeists have come to grief there, the latest a honeymooning couple. An unmarked stone is their memorial.

A small pile of stones some ten miles from the coast commemorates the murder of two missionary priests at Bloody Falls. In November of 1913, due to misunderstanding, two Eskimos believed their lives were threatened by the missionaries. The Natives killed them. It took two lengthy trials in Alberta to reach the verdict of guilty. These were the first Inuit Eskimos tried under the white man's law.

Bloody Falls was a favorite spot for ambush in the centuries-old hostility between Indians and Eskimos. Hearne could do nothing to stop the massacre his Indian companions inflicted on the sleeping Eskimos.

The falls is really triple rapids, dropping more than ninety feet. Even expert canoeists portage around the foaming water, and we noticed a dented aluminum canoe on the high bank. Its paddlers had become disheartened, abandoned their craft, and walked to Coppermine.

A lone person (left) is dwarfed by Bloody Falls' canyon.

We portaged on the plateau 450 to 600 feet above the rapids, mentally selecting a possible pathway through those fierce waves. But our leader, Charlie Third, a vocational guidance teacher from Pembroke, Ontario, prudently decided against the notion.

"We'd take too much water over the bow, and it's still ice-cold, you know. We'd all be ready for pneumonia before we reached that little beach."

The roar of the rapids deafened us as it had the Eskimos long ago. Fish still thronged the pools. Ducks waddled on the silt islands, and golden eagles sat sentry on twiggy nests above the water.

All hands took to the paddles as the river wound sluggishly through the coastal plain to the islanded Coronation Gulf (named by Franklin to commemorate the crowning of the Prince Regent as George IV, King of England) and the settlement of Coppermine.

The village has grown slowly to a population of 900. In addition to the familiar features of an Arctic settlement, there is now an Inuit Co-op store. We surged to its handicrafts section, and some guests polished off their Christmas shopping four months early.

"You should come by every week," giggled the pretty young Inuit clerk.

FOR FURTHER INFORMATION:

Arctic Waterways
R.R. # 2
Stevensville, Ontario
Canada L0S 1S0
Phone (416) 382-3882

South Nahanni River
NORTHWEST TERRITORIES

On the northwestern edge of the great prairies, between the Mackenzie River and the Mackenzie Mountains (the border between Yukon Territory and the Northwest Territories), runs the South Nahanni River of sinister repute. It meanders in places, building silt islands; ripples around bends; then surges through four mighty canyons in a muddy swirl to join the Liard ("poplar"), the Mackenzie's largest tributary.

What did we know of this remote, lonely river, apart from some sinister place-names — Deadmen Valley, Funeral Range, Headless Valley? . . . Few people had ever been there. Even the name, Nahanni, is a corruption of a Slavey Indian word meaning faraway. We had heard of its awesome canyons, of its waterfall nearly twice the height of Niagara, of tropical valleys and gold nuggets and mysterious deaths. Only a few prospectors and trappers, a handful of park officials, a few canoeists and some rafting enthusiasts had been over the route. Like them, we came from the south.

Dan Culver, proprietor of Whitewater Adventures in Vancouver, held the sole right to commercial rafting on the Nahanni. He learned his rafting skills on the foaming rivers of British Columbia. Blonde hair bleached white from his outdoor life, he waited at the seaplane dock of Watson Lake (Mile 611 of the Alaska Highway) with his crew of three. Randy had been with Dan for several seasons; Kirk had canoed down the river the previous year, and respected its rapids and eddies; and far from least, Sandy was Dan's lady-partner and superlative cook.

There were seventeen of us eager rafters plus the crew, three deflated rafts (each weighing close to two hundred pounds), and a young mountain of gear and provisions to feed twenty-one people for twelve days. We were willing to help with loading the plane, but Dan and the pilot declined with thanks. It would take two flights to accommodate everything and everyone. The sun turned the spray of the pontoons into rainbows, then the Otter soared up and over the surrounding hills.

In turn, we winged over the Mackenzie Mountains to the head of the South Nahanni National Park, threaded along the river. We traversed the Ragged Range of high, sharp peaks through a notch called Hole-in-the-Wall. These hard black granite peaks, a notable challenge to climbers, form the park's northern boundary.

This wilderness area of more than three thousand square miles was set aside in 1972, proclaimed four years later, and in 1978 was admitted to the select company of United Nations Heritage Properties (like the Pyramids and the Colorado River), to be maintained

The uniquely terraced Rabbitkettle Hot Springs are a short walk from the Nahanni.

by Canada as a near-pristine region, uncluttered by roads, residences, airstrips or marinas, held in trust for future generations.

The plane lost altitude and, looking down, we could discern the river, tawny with silt, uncoiling below. Its serpentine curves were studded with self-made bars and islands. The plane skidded to a halt, nuzzling close to a sheer silt bank carved by the river. Now everyone helped with the unloading and stacking and raft-inflating, eager to set out on 210 miles of rafting down to Nahanni Butte, where our river joined the Liard.

We passengers were a diverse lot: a doctor and a dentist (both women), a semi-retired California space engineer, a teacher of electronics, a jovial fellow from Ontario who admitted to weighing 275 pounds, and a young man from Rhode Island who, in spite of cerebral palsy, proved himself a meticulous camper and did more than his share of the rowing. All were in reasonably good physical condition.

Like all rafters we wore life jackets, but in the calm stretches we bent the rules and stripped to the waist to soak up the sun. The hordes of early summer mosquitoes were finished by now. We carried no gasoline, for motors are not allowed in this park except for use by park wardens. While we worked, the park ranger for this section brought his family across the river to look us over and sell fishing licenses at four

A rainbow arcs over the Nahanni near Virginia Falls.

dollars a clip. He also took our names and addresses, a wise precaution on a notoriously dangerous river.

We didn't need a motor anyway, for the current carried us along in some places at the rate of forty miles in a short day. We guided the rafts by rowing occasionally, and paddles were provided for any who cared to use them. That first afternoon, we exuberantly hoisted an oar as a mast and tied on a tent fly to act as a spinnaker sail.

A belted kingfisher racketed off downstream, and a caribou swam across the river before we pushed off in the sunny afternoon. Our shakedown cruise lasted only an hour or so, bringing us to the Rabbitkettle River, where we scrambled onto a narrow beach imprinted with the tracks of bear, wolf, beaver and moose. In time

A red makeshift spinnaker *(top)* frames the high cliffs of the Nahanni. Rafters *(above)* observe a moose.

we became quite accustomed to such a variety of spoor, as it appeared on many small beaches. The animals themselves kept discreetly out of sight.

We had learned that hot springs occurred at several locations along the river, both in and outside the park — the final manifestations of the earth's crusty energy and the resulting "tropical valleys." But we were not prepared for two spectacular mounds. The North Mound measured nearly ninety feet high and three times that in diameter at the base. Each mound was shaped like a many-layered wedding cake, or a terraced Asian rice field. A crystal pool on the top of each mound steamed sulfurously, and water at 70 °F welled up and over the rim, cooled, and precipitated calcium carbonate tufa. The warm water spilled down rimmed terraces that overbrimmed and created new terraces. Because of pedestrian damage to the fragile tufa, the mounds are now closed to the public, but you can still wade Hole-in-the-Wall Creek, follow an overgrown path for a mile, and gaze upon these unique formations.

That night the aurora borealis blazed overhead, to the awe and delight of the Californians who had never before observed the northern lights. Beside the leaping campfire a camper recited the racy ballad "The Cremation of Sam McGee," by Yukon poet Robert Service.

A following wind carried us smartly downstream the next day, and at night we pitched our tents across from Sunblood Mountain. I noticed a tremor of the earth and a continuous low grumble as I lay on the ground in my sleeping bag.

"That's Virginia Falls!" exclaimed my tentmate. "We'll be there soon."

The lonely falls signal their location not only by steady pounding but also by the high banner of spume. In one place you can look over the brink and see matchsticks strewn 316 feet below. They are really full-size trees. The quiet river hurries in white-edged waves in the Sluice-box before leaping the precipice and splitting around a 300-foot steeple of rock. The Slavey Indians called the cataract *Nali-chuk* (Big Drop), a name more apt than the one it bears.

It took about half an hour to portage around the falls, everyone carrying as much as possible. The trail was actually the ancient riverbed, the lowest and steepest end of the ancient precipice. The sky darkened suddenly in the swift change of weather familiar on the Nahanni, and hail pelted down, beating so hard on my unprotected head that I dived for the shelter of a big pine. For ten minutes I stood there with an armful of paddles while ice pellets bounced two feet off the ground, leaving millions of ice marbles on the mucky trail.

Down below, while the crew re-inflated the rafts, I climbed over boulders full of fossils to get a close-up

All ashore for a picnic lunch on the banks of the Nahanni.

Golden sunshine lights up the rocks of Second Canyon.

At 316 feet high, Virginia Falls presents a barrier that Nahanni rafters must portage around.

view of Virginia Falls, where 100,000 cubic feet of water per second leaped over the cliff. So dense was the downpour of the condensed spray that I was soon drenched. At first I walked in mist, then in spray, then in a downpour so solid I couldn't see ten feet ahead. When I turned back, a quarter-mile from the thunderous cascade, I was soaking wet.

That afternoon we pushed off again in full sunlight. The rocky entrance to Five-Mile Canyon glowed yellow-brown-orange as the river twisted through five miles of fast water between steep banks, but we rode as buoyant as gulls and easily avoided standing waves a yard high. It seemed to us that we shot through the canyon, to land at Marengo Creek campground.

A porcupine stopped nibbling bark to stare at us, then backed down the tree and, quills rattling, made off into the bush. We noticed that the wooden outdoor privy (the only one we encountered on the trip) had been gnawed by our prickly friend. We made sure that our sweat-salted paddles and oars were out of its reach that night.

At breakfast next morning our enjoyment of the wilderness was interrupted by the chatter of a helicopter and of a motorboat coming upstream. Both landed near us. We were affronted that our serenity had been invaded. What were they doing here?

The motorboat had brought up bags of cement for a cairn above Virginia Falls, on which a metal plaque would mark the South Nahanni Park as a UNESCO-protected Heritage Property. The helicopter had come to deliver building materials above the falls, including a brand-new privy for officials and newsmen at the dedication ceremony. The helicopter churned above us, the biffy dangling on a cable. It was the chance of a lifetime to see a flying toilet!

This so occupied our attention that no one attempted the bushwack trail to the quadruple falls six miles up the creek.

Instead we hastened downriver. We saw a young moose swimming a channel where the Flat River entered. Some rafters have been lucky in seeing "a total of 30 Dall sheep, 3-4 black bears, a beaver swimming the river, one woodland caribou, the non-herding variety, a mother duck swimming upriver, her family strung out behind, one wolf."

The current, always swift, speeds up as the river plunges into the Third and the Second canyons. (Trappers coming up from the Liard labeled the canyons simply in the order they met. We met them in reverse.)

Together these two canyons through Funeral Range total thirty-five miles. About halfway along, a favorite lunch stop is a narrow shingle at the foot of Pulpit Rock, a free-standing sentinel six hundred feet high. We climbed the lower shale slopes. Immediately beyond is the Gate, where the South Nahanni makes a hair-pin turn and is constricted to one hundred feet, below cliffs 1,400 feet high. The swift water is variously named "the rapid that runs both ways," "Hell's Gate" and the "Figure 8 Rapid." The river slams into the rock wall and piles up a standing wave two yards high, flanked on both sides by seething whirlpools. It is definitely Class V at high water levels, but was deep and quiet for us. We spun our rafts in the eddies just for fun.

When we emerged from Second Canyon, the land spread out in the wide, beautiful Deadmen Valley. We pitched our tents high above the river (for the water level can rise ten feet in four hours in the canyons) near an unoccupied ranger cabin. It was a lovely site with a panoramic view of the Prairie Creek delta, a silt fan with a salt lick nearby, beloved of the mountain sheep. Across the Nahanni was Dry Canyon and, downstream, the entrance to spectacular First Canyon.

At dinner we ate our anglers' graylings as appetizers, and kidded our exploring party for having lost their way in Dry Canyon. Kirk had camped here last year, and around the campfire he told the saga of Deadmen Valley, stripped of purple prose.

His tale in brief: "In 1905 two brothers named McLeod, trappers from Fort Liard, struggled up the Nahanni to Flat River, where they found a few small nuggets of gold, not enough to start even a mini-rush. They started back home, but never got there. A search party three years later found their camp here and their skeletons, all but the skulls. They buried the bones and

Pulpit Rock (left) gets a long look from guests who have stopped at the gateway to Second Canyon. The wall of First Canyon (above) dwarfs a raft.

59

Rafters enjoy a soak in Kraus Hot Springs' sulfurous water.

beyond that, rimmed by still higher mountains. The height increases a little each year, for the river continues to carve its trough deeper at the rate of two yards every thousand years. The river is older than the surrounding hills. They rose up after the watercourse was formed, "like butter rising around a crooked knife," as one ranger put it.

We neither paddled nor rowed — simply drifted — through the silted, minute particles in this awesome trench, following the current from wall to wall.

Immediately out of the canyon, a wind blowing upriver brought to our nostrils a stench of rotten eggs, indicating our approach to the sulferous Kraus Hot Springs. Prospector-trapper Gus Kraus and his wife Mary lived here intermittently from 1940 to 1971. When the national park was being laid out, they chose to move to a small, fish-filled lake. They left behind the garden that grew luxuriantly in the warm steamy atmosphere, a vegetable garden that was the marvel of the Nahanni. The vigorous growth and the variety of vegetation reinforced the legend of a tropical valley, but there never were any palms or bananas.

We rafters trooped through their fields of timothy hay, of dillweed and parsnips and other self-seeded relics of the Kraus's green fingers. A stream, varicolored with algae, drained a large pond that steamed in the drizzly air. Ignoring the foul smell and the blobs of green waterweed and the muddy bottom, we stripped to underclothes and submerged in the 90°F warmth of the springs. The sense of well-being outlasted the light rain.

Once out of the canyon, the uncorseted river spreads in a welter of silt islands and channels called the Splits, and leaves the borders of the national park.

Some ten miles from the hot springs rises a solitary knob of reddish rock, Nahanni Butte. The Slavey Indian village of the same name nestles at its foot — a dozen log cabins strung out along the riverbank, clustered close to a trading post that sold handicraft items.

And there two floatplanes waited to wing us back to the town of Watson Lake. We boarded reluctantly. After two weeks of "getting away from it all," we had to leave the serenity of the river for the dust of the Alaska Highway.

FOR FURTHER INFORMATION:

Whitewater Adventures
1511 Anderson Street
Granville Island
Vancouver, British Columbia
Canada V6H 3R5
Phone (604) 669-1100

named this valley 'Deadmen'. All kinds of lurid stories were told of mysterious wild mountain men, and reporters coined the name Headless Valley. But the Royal Canadian Mounted Police figured the brothers died of hunger and exposure, and wild beasts scattered the bones."

Someone quoted from Ray Patterson's classic, *The Dangerous River.*

Downriver began the 22-mile First Canyon, the most dramatic spot on the Nahanni. Its hard limestone walls rise sheer for 3,500 feet, and the Nahanni Plateau lifts

13

Firth River
YUKON TERRITORY

Still farther north runs the Firth River, named for a staunch Hudson's Bay Company factor. Robert Firth served the company at various trading posts in the extreme northwest of Canada, married a pretty girl of the Loucheux tribe, and fathered a quiverful of children.

What Canadian river could be more remote from city traffic than the Firth, high in the peak of Yukon Territory? Rafters on that river might well feel like explorers, for every curve would be a new experience. Only a handful have run its course.

That's how Jim Lavalley of Vancouver reasoned when casting about for a river sufficiently unfamiliar. He found his untraveled river when some experienced canoeists admitted the Firth had defeated them.

"It's full of ledges and rapids," they said, "and canyons that nearly meet overhead. It rises in Alaska, crosses into the Yukon, and runs through the Barrens. After about 120 miles it hits the Beaufort Sea."

A raft can take waters too dangerous for a canoe, Jim had learned, and the Firth became his river of dreams. In 1981 he and a small exploring party prospected his proposed raft route successfully to the Arctic Ocean.

Reflection in Jim Lavalley's dark glasses spells Hyak, the name of his company.

The canyon of the Firth cuts through the pale green Barrens.

Lavalley weighed the distance against the allure of faraway places, and decided the expense would not deter ardent rafters. He and his wife, Julie (met on a raft trip), set up Hyak ("fast water" in the Chinook jargon) River Expeditions.

It was still adventurous rafting for passengers on subsequent runs. Jim had learned the techniques and logistics of rafting from "Big John" Mikes of Vancouver, "the father of Canadian river rafting," who set a high level of comfort and cookery. Distances never bothered Mikes nor his disciples. That very remoteness was a major attraction.

Thus we ten passengers — two consulting engineers and their wives, the owner of a New York radio station, a couple of photographers — met the crew of four in

Whitehorse, capital of the Yukon, and flew in a chartered DC-3 to the Loucheux Indian village of Old Crow. The neat log houses there are strung out between the airstrip and the Porcupine River.

An Otter floatplane was moored at the little dock, and the gear from the DC-3 was quickly transferred, all lending a hand. However, supplies for ten days for fourteen people, plus those bodies and three rolled eight-by-eighteen-foot rafts, could not be shoehorned into the Otter. Two trips would be necessary.

Several veteran rafters went in the first load with our gear, and Jim joked, "I'll tuck you fellows in and come back for the rest."

North of the village sprawled the immense area of Old Crow Flats, notable not only for muskrat pelts but

A natural flowerbed *(left)* of willow herb adorns the beach in front of a tent. Two rafts *(above)* drift through one of the long rock canyons of the lower Firth.

for anthropological finds of prehistoric man, giant beavers and wild oxen.

A hundred miles north we sighted the Firth River, winding clear and green through a landscape that was grand rather than pretty. A large pond, Lake Margaret, lay only a few yards from the river. Here the pilot set the Otter down in a rainbow spray, swiftly unloaded, and hurried back for the second contingent.

In spite of bright sun at midnight we slept at once, not even waking for the second arrival of the plane. We roused only when a quiet voice murmured, "How do you like your eggs cooked?" No one demanded Eggs Benedict until later on the trip, and no one protested that first morning when they were served poached,

dripping with Hollandaise sauce. Jim had learned gourmet cookery under Big John Mikes, and was training his crew in turn.

Thus every evening before dinner he set out red and white wine as apertifs, and we helped ourselves. The entrée might be steak, butterflied pork chops, shish kebab or spicy stew. It hardly ever rains on the Firth, but one night it happened, and we had dinner of barbecued spareribs and strawberry shortcake for breakfast.

It was amazing what luscious meals those styrofoam hampers yielded, and what blue-plate cooks those boatmen became. Not only were they proficient in service, but endlessly patient with our queries. One was an ornithologist from Carleton University, Ottawa, who identified more than fifty bird species within the ten days, including eider ducks, golden eagles, swans and peregrine falcons.

We all loafed that first day, catching up on sleep, getting acquainted with our fellow travelers and with our setting. We were tenting in a veritable flowerbed of short-stemmed blossoms eager to set seed in the long sunshine. A guest from California consulted her handbook, and named forty-five species along the river,

including cerise willow herb, hairy avens and pink fleabane. I cut a slice off a five-inch log of firewood to count the growth rings: 150 before they became too narrow for my magnifying glass — 150 years a-growing on that Arctic coast!

The river, not dusk, lulled us to sleep at night, and hurtled us seaward by day through long, deep canyons whose sheer rock faces had been twisted by primordial convulsions into undulating bands and anticlines. At times the cold green water slid down a mile or so in rapids. We dashed through back-curling waves, shipping spray and water over our scarlet life jackets. At intervals the river leaped down rocky ledges four or five feet high — falls that had to be approached with skill, cornering our blunt bows into the waves.

From the safety of our rafts we observed the occasional cinnamon bear ambling down a slope to drink from our river. An Arctic wolf, drinking, was vastly surprised when these noiseless monsters floated by, invading his solitude. High up, a family of Dall sheep posed like white statuettes on an inaccessible crag. Once we spotted a couple of caribou in the distance, outside camera range — stragglers from the Porcupine Herd, eighty to a hundred thousand strong.

"I just hope we catch the herd swimming the river in their annual migration. That's the spectacle I'm after," said the photographer from Vancouver.

Yet caribou are capricious. Some whim or alarm causes a band to desert traditional migration routes, so hunger strikes Indians, Inuit Eskimos, and even explorers. We soon found evidence that caribou had crossed the river a week before, for molted hairs lay in small windrows on shore.

The last vestiges of trees dwindled and vanished as we floated through the Barren Grounds. The river changed from a single course to a wide fan of streamlets, a delta typical of the rivers crossing the flat shoreline of the Beaufort Sea. Many channels were already shrunken after the spring runoff, and our air-inflated rafts touched bottom too often for peace of mind.

Some guests go topless, even two hundred miles above the Arctic Circle.

Rafters push clear of ice pans at the mouth of the Firth River.

Jim Lavalley balanced his six-foot three-inch frame on the dunnage for a better view in choosing the best channels, but before long all three rafts were grounded. We could smell the salt in the breeze, and even see whitecaps on the dark blue sea beyond a long sandpit.

One after another we stepped out of our rafts into the icy water. It was cold, hard work, and as so often happens, it provoked gallows humor. Quips were hurled back and forth, and laughter gurgled in our throats. Beyond all logic, it was fun. And successful, for we reached the end of the spit, and a gentle wave lifted us over. The wave was salty, and now we could discern that the whitecaps were really solid cakes of ice.

We had reached the Arctic Ocean. That evening Jim didn't set out the usual wine, but instead celebratory champagne. The sandspit was cluttered with thousands of logs cut in the Mackenzie delta more than one hundred miles to the east and carried west by wind and current. Having lacked firewood in the Barrens, we now had an abundance and we fed our campfire with joyous abandon.

Dinner was late that night, but the butterflied pork chops were worth waiting for. We sat long, bathed in sunset colors, only the sun didn't set. It hovered near the horizon, then rose again while we marveled. Around us whirled flocks of snow buntings, and trumpeter swans winged overhead.

During the night the wind shifted and drove the ice cakes toward shore, so our boatmen had difficulty launching the rafts. That same wind carried the rafts west toward our takeout place near Komakuk, Canada's most westerly DEWline station, where we had a rendezvous with our DC-3, 220 miles above the Arctic Circle.

When the wind changed and the boatmen had to row, some of us welcomed the chance to stretch our legs. It was pleasant walking the beach in the hazy sunshine, with the white domes of the station acting as a beacon.

And when we reached the station, our photographer clutched his hair in frustration when they told him, "Caribou! You should have been here last week. We had 'em everywhere, thousands of them."

Caribou are notoriously unpredictable. But that was our single disappointment. We all agreed that this rafting experience, entirely above the Arctic Circle, was the greatest in the Northwest.

FOR FURTHER INFORMATION:

Jim Lavalley
Hyak River Expeditions Inc.
1416 West 5th Avenue
Vancouver, British Columbia
Canada V6J 1N8
Phone (604) 734-8622

Tatshenshini River
BRITISH COLUMBIA • YUKON • ALASKA

The Tatshenshini, racing across the Yukon, British Columbia and Alaska, is not so long as that would suggest. It's an ideal river for rafting, although it's a long way off for most adventurers.

The rafting itself covers only 175 watery miles through scenery that mounts in splendor. But the whole package involves several modes of transportation, beginning with the coastal state ferry from Juneau, Alaska to Haines at the head of the Lynn Canal. You get a noble view of the snowcapped Coast Range all the way.

The scenic Haines access road, based on an ancient Indian trail and the horse-and-cattle road hacked out by the redoubtable Jack Dalton during the Klondike gold rush, calls for a minibus to Mile 110, once Dalton's Post. Five bumpy miles off the Haines, we came to "our" river.

While awaiting our arrival the boatmen had pumped up the four eighteen-foot neoprene rafts ready for tomorrow's launching. They even set up our green tents, to break us in gradually, and prepared the first of twelve gourmet dinners.

Not only were the young men skilled at the oars, but they were chefs of no mean order. They were trained by John Mikes, formerly a Czech hotelier, and originator of rafting trips in Canada. Dinner was always a feast, preceded by drinks on the house.

Lunch was a simple do-it-yourself assemblage from various breads and spreads, cookies and fruit laid out on a clean board. Breakfast was worth getting up for when the aroma of camp coffee reached your tent. There was always bacon or sausage plus eggs in various forms, porridge, and often blueberry hotcakes.

The tumultous fast water of the upper river dawdles as it traverses silt and gravel flats, where its innumerable channels create islands that change in shape with every freshet. We found many tracks of

In warm sunshine, rafters enjoy a quiet stretch of the Tatshenshini.

beaver and bear in the wet silt. I measured one of an Alaskan brown bear near my tent at eighteen inches. We were all glad to be informed that this largest of bears is timid, avoiding confrontations.

Still, any shore hikes are accompanied by a staff man toting a rifle, happily never needed to date. We saw only one bear, a small grizzly.

Our four rafts, each with six occupants, bounced over waves that any canoeist would respect, and floated over shallow riffles where the boatmen merely needed to keep the rafts in the current. From time to time other rivers flowed in, notably the Takhanne after a glorious leap down the mountainside, and the Alsek, surging in through a maze of islands to engulf the Tatshenshini.

One island was completely covered with nesting gulls. Water ouzels dipped their tails amusingly, while sandpipers and phalaropes waded in the shallows. Tiny, dark hummingbirds were fascinated by our scarlet life jackets, and bald eagles screamed annoyance at our intrusion.

Off to the east, where the British Columbia-Alaska border is particularly irregular, rises Mount Fairweather, rearing above the other noble peaks, at 15,320 feet the highest in the province of British Columbia. It, like many another in the magnificent Coast Range, is draped with glaciers.

At one bend of the river, now the Alsek, I counted fourteen glaciers at once, some of them still unnamed.

We halted near Walker Glacier and scrambled over a field of moraine gravel to walk on the lip of the advancing ice mass. The crystalline surface rose slightly to the face of the bizarre-shaped ice that towered above us. We had to pick a careful way between deep crevasses and sinister-looking holes where meltwater swirled as it carved a subsurface path to the river.

I felt a peculiar exhilaration in trudging over that rough, ancient — almost prehistoric — ice. Warmed by the sun, we perched on rocks that had been buried in ice for centuries but now had surfaced and were being borne gradually into the river.

Of our twelve days on the river, only one proved too rainy for pleasure, as we neared the coast. We eighteen guests voted a lay-over within our snug tents, to read and visit back and forth. Tomorrow might bring better

Masses of ice *(facing page, far left)* greet a group of guests who hiked to the foot of a glacier. Magnificent scenery *(facing page)* surrounds rafters on the Alsek River. A raft *(left)* approaches a glacier as close as is prudent.

weather. The boatmen-chefs laid on an especially appetizing dinner, which we ate al fresco as usual but under the protection of a tarpaulin supported by oars.

We were glad we had dallied when next morning the low rain clouds yielded to a brilliant day, in which the glaciers seemed to have moved in closer. We saw them close-up at Alsek Bay.

The bay is a large pouch on the left bank of the Tatshenshini-Alsek, a lagoon filled with icebergs. The Alsek Glacier, three miles wide, calves constantly. We could see the fall of hundreds of tons of ice, and seconds later hear the roar of splitting and the crash into the water. Then came the waves, to rock our rafts though we dared not approach closer than a quarter-mile. The large bergs held caverns of blue ice, results of trapped oxygen.

We moored our rafts to a small berg and assembled our lunch from the usual tasty layout, entertained all the while by the glacier's action.

Then the clouds moved in again from the Pacific, now only thirty miles to the west, and we had to locate our final campsite. We each set up our tent, pumped up our air mattress and spread our sleeping bag (all leased) for our last night on the river.

Next morning, two small airplanes kept their rendezvous with us at Dry Bay, and we were off on the last leg of our rafting holiday. An eighty-minute flight to Juneau climbed above the glaciers, which we now perceived to be brown-and-white striped ribbons of dirt-encrusted ice.

It was the end of the most scenic rafting in North America.

FOR FURTHER INFORMATION:

**Canadian River Expeditions
845 Chilco Street
Vancouver, British Columbia
Canada V6G 2R2
Phone (604) 738-4449**

**Sobek Expeditions Inc.
Box 1007
Angels Camp, California
U.S.A. 95222
Phone (209) 736-4524
     (800) 344-3284**

The Mountains

The young (geologically speaking) Rocky Mountain Range forms most of the boundary between the provinces of Alberta and British Columbia, the western bracket of the prairies, and the eastern bracket of the great cordillera that fills most of Canada's Pacific province. Between the snowcapped Rockies and the glacier-draped Coast Range rises a parallel series of lesser ranges alternating with deep, narrow trenches, all spawning creeks and rivers in a hurry to reach the Pacific.

Fog, drizzle and rain are frequent on the Skeena, one of the rivers of the great Rocky Mountain Range.

15

Kicking Horse River
BRITISH COLUMBIA

"Go with the flow" is the slogan of the enterprising young men who launched the Kicking Horse Rafting Company of Golden, British Columbia.

This swift river grows from trickles in the ice cap nestling in the mountain peaks, and rampages westward to join the Columbia at the town of Golden.

Mike Williams instructs students who are learning to raft on the turbulent Kicking Horse.

The river acquired its peculiar name from a dramatic accident of 1858. Young Dr. James Hector, a Scots geologist, had found this pass after months of surveying. As he rode through the brawling stream, the cayuse stumbled and threw his rider. In the struggle to regain his balance, the horse kicked the young man in the head and knocked him unconscious. He was taken for dead. A grave was hastily dug beside the river, the body was laid in the grave, and men stood poised to shovel earth over it. By a mighty effort the presumed corpse blinked one eyelid, and the burial stopped on the spot. The name remains.

When the Canadian Pacific Railway engineers sought a way through the Continental Divide, they finally chose Kicking Horse Pass in spite of severe inclines and an altitude of nearly five thousand feet.

The upper reaches of the river are too rocky and too turbulent for rafting, but Mike Williams of Golden, who was running a daily training course in river rafting, took me along for the day. Mike was a small man, bearded, with a hoarse voice ("from shouting at my trainees").

We drove twelve or fifteen miles east of Golden on the Trans-Canada Highway to the edge of Yoho National Park, then down a steep track to the Kicking Horse River. The cold green water boiled along. High up, across twenty to thirty yards of racing river, gleamed

the shining steel rails of the C.P.R. main line, where long freight trains pulled hoppers of wheat coastward.

The students were already gathered as we coasted down the dirt track. All were Canadians, from far and near, including one girl from Thunder Bay, Ontario, with short blond hair in stubby braids. Claire was deter-mined to keep up with her boyfriend, and together they were assembling the frameworks of three rafts. Some students were new and clumsy, others slick after a few lessons.

Mike explained that the students neither pay tuition fees nor get paid for taking guests on the river. His

Hung up on a rock, a rafting student studies the situation.

73

Students learn safety techniques before rafting the Kicking Horse.

Two students observe others shooting a rapid.

FOR FURTHER INFORMATION:

Kicking Horse Rafting Co. Ltd.
Box 1890
Golden, British Columbia
Canada V0A 1H0
Phone (604) 344-5729
(403) 762-5627

Glacier Raft Company
Box 219
Radium Hot Springs, British Columbia
Canada V0A 1M0
Phone (604) 347-9218

curriculum included rowing — this is no river for amateur paddlers, but rather a "Mexican motor" (oars, that is). One boatman with a pair of sweeps controls the movement of the raft. "Kicking Horse is a very technical river," Mike averred. "That is, one with plenty of challenge."

Today the students were to learn how to run a heavy technical rapid. A stretch of boisterous water romped in front of Mike and a trainee as they studied the flow among the boulders. He had to shout to make himself heard over the roar of the rapids. "Holes" (hydraulics) must be avoided if possible. Then Mike went along with each student, shouting further instructions. All the trainees made the run successfully, though Claire got hung up on a submerged rock. The current, however, turned her raft, and she swung off in a complete round-about — facing upstream!

The students and Mike ran different sections of the river for about four hours. Passing locomotive engineers and brakemen, as well as section-gangs, craned for a good look and waved. Four mountain goats stared with no visible emotion, and two bald-headed eagles couldn't have cared less.

I had been bailing a lot of water out of Mike's raft from my perch at the front, while a student sat in the stern. We pulled out at a small gravel beach, and the students were instructed how to handle a guest — even to helping this one across slippery rocks. Preparing lunch was another lesson, and one on first aid seemed timely when a young man gashed his hand on a sharp rock.

By the time Mike would graduate these students, he could qualify them as certified river guides, proficient in all the rafting arts. They would be snapped up by outfitters on rivers across the country, including two on this very river.

My experience came in middle water level, the ideal time, though the season stretches from mid-June to mid-August. A spell of warm weather can melt icecaps and increase the flow dramatically. Or a prolonged rainy season may swell the runoff, so rafting may be halted by reason of too much violent water rather than too little. "We go with the flow," Mike quoted with a grin.

He paid me the honor of inviting me to raft his "own private river," the Spillamacheen. But our mutual schedules did not permit — not then, anyway.

Kootenay River
BRITISH COLUMBIA

The fast waters of the East Kootenay Valley attract rafters as the steep slopes attract skiers and the hot springs attract bathers.

Several companies raft the Kootenay, one at least of them, Glacier Raft Company, also running the Kicking Horse (see preceding chapter).

Threading through the Kootenay National Park, the Kootenay River burbles south to the Montana border, where it changes its spelling to Kootenai. Both are anglicized spellings of an old Kutenay Indian word.

The lively character of the river has been tamed in its lower reaches by a series of high dams, and the lovely mountain and savannah scenery invaded by enormous hydroelectric pylons marching across the land like giantesses, arms akimbo.

The road from Banff penetrates the mountain wall through the flaming red rock of Sinclair Canyon. Then one comes to Radium Hot Springs and its village. Headquarters of the Kootenay River Runners is a step farther north at Edgewater.

But Radium is the start for one- or two-day trips downriver. Day trips encompass about thirty miles of the lovely river, with a maximum of six to a raft. Overnight trips take in some forty-five miles of river. Larger rafts are used, accommodating ten to fourteen plus their gear.

Daryl Bespflug *(left)* owns and operates Kootenay River Runners. The put-in place *(above)* for Kootenay rafting is in Kootenay National Park.

75

Rafters enjoy the splendid scenery of the Kootenay National Park.

Promptly at 10 A.M., head boatman Daryl Bespflug arrived in his minibus, towing a single eighteen-foot inflated Havasu raft, and with him half-a-dozen passengers, all from Calgary, all taking a holiday.

Daryl quickly drove us 14 miles back into Kootenay National Park, to Settlers' Road, which led us to where the blue-green waters of the Kootenay River rippled south, dropping about 350 feet in the 45 miles. He supplied the usual life jackets, voluminous rubber pants and yellow waterproof slickers. His helper drove the minibus back home, and would meet us at the takeout place at the end of our trip next day.

Rafting was a novel experience to half the crowd, and they sat forward somewhat timidly, but eagerly scanning the passing scenery — all but a thirteen-year-old boy, who wearied the adults with his endless complaining and comments. "Can't we go any faster?" "Wish we had a car." No one pushed him overboard despite the temptation. But we had a forty-foot lifeline coiled at Daryl's feet, ready for instant action.

Lois, the boy's mother, was deathly afraid of bugs and bears, but was thrilled to be the first to sight a three-year-old bear, which quickly ambled off into the bush. So did a young buck with tiny antlers. We paused to explore an abandoned cabin, kept clean by the canoeists who made use of it.

The river wavered in and out of the national park. We spotted eagles, ospreys, swallows and wild ducks. We took splashes in medium waves (Grades II to IV) and a few more in the afternoon after lunch on a gravel bar at the mouth of Cross River. Violets and wild strawberries were in bloom.

Daryl rows hard to bring the raft close to a waterfall.

Around five o'clock we pulled out at another gravel bar, carried our gear well up from the river, and set up our tents wherever we chose. This was a semi-permanent campsite of Daryl, who held the franchise for rafting in Kootenay National Park. By now he had made more than four hundred trips on the river, including half-day trips. He also rafts the Kicking Horse and Toby Creek.

Besides rafting, Daryl guides ocean kayaking trips in Baja, California when the wind blows chill from the Rocky Mountain icecaps. In between times, he satisfies his wanderlust by long bicycle trips. No doubt he was "born on a goosefeather bed, and thus bound to roam."

The river murmured softly through the long twilight, and a bird called melodiously. "A ruby-crowned kinglet," announced Daryl, who knew his birds by sight and by sound.

He cooked dinner over the low campfire. As his brochure claimed, the food at noon was like a deli-catessen, and the T-bone steak dinner merited the quip, "Float and bloat."

The large steak (too big for me) was flanked by stir-fried fresh vegetables and hot garlic bread, and followed by luscious Black Forest cake. I had to walk it off on a narrow game trail above the rushing river. Snow peaks of the Selkirk Mountains rose to the west, and beneath my feet were the brick-red rocks peculiar to this area of the Kootenay.

Later we sat around the campfire on logs and drew from Daryl some reminiscences of his world travels — anecdotes of his long bicycle tours in remote parts of the world, in Asia and South America.

I woke to the familiar honk of a raven. From beyond came the trill of the kinglet. The tiny gray bird sang from the top of a lodgepole pine, his scarlet headpatch raised in a crest.

Mingled with the fragrance of pine and hemlock, and overwhelming the scent of wild roses, came the aroma of camp coffee, sizzling bacon and last night's leftover potatoes being pan-fried, plus pancakes from a Men-

Daryl *(below)* prepares sourdough pancakes for breakfast. Dense forest and ice-topped peaks *(right)* flank the Kootenay River.

FOR FURTHER INFORMATION:

Kootenay River Runners
Box 81
Edgewater, British Columbia
Canada V0A 1E0
Phone (604) 347-9210

Glacier Raft Company
Box 219
Radium Hot Springs, British Columbia
Canada V0A 1M0
Phone (604) 347-9218

nonite mix called Coyote. A howling success, to coin a pun.

On our way again, we paused at a wide whitewater cascade tumbling into the Kootenay. You can rarely maneuver backward in a raft to get a better view, so we all trooped ashore through a resinous pine wood to see another aspect of Pedley Falls, and discovered to our regret that the treed banks of our river were simply an "illusion swath," a mere hedge screening the hillside devastated by loggers.

"The law says a fringe of trees must be left, to preserve the view," Daryl explained. "But in this cynical world it's more profitable to cut everything, then pay the government the stipulated low fine."

By 3 P.M. we reached a disused logging bridge. There the minibus waited, an end to our exhilarating hours on the Kootenay.

Rafting trip ends at a logging road, where transportation back to Radium Hot Springs awaits.

17

Toby Creek
BRITISH COLUMBIA

Not everyone likes — or is suited to — lengthy rafting adventures. For many newcomers a one-day trip or even a couple of hours afloat is all they crave. *Vive la différence!*

While floating down the Kootenay I learned of several other short trips in the area, such as on the Blaeberry, which flows into the Columbia north of Golden. And, closer to hand, on Toby Creek.

This is a short, fast stream, originating in Toby Lake and charging eastward down the slope of 9,600-foot Mount Toby, one of the snow-crowned peaks of the Purcell Range of the Selkirks. It joins the Kootenay at the resort town of Invermere.

I met a group of twenty-four oil company employees, who had driven south of Radium Hot Springs for the outing. A Calgary group, all sported blue peaked caps bearing the company name. Was the excursion a business bonus or a sudden vacation-time impulse?

By midafternoon we all climbed aboard a bus and slowly wound up a mountain road for five miles

A school bus and a flatbed loaded with rafts stop on a logging road beside Toby Creek.

Day trippers are instructed in safety rules.

79

through fields of wild lupine, Indian paintbrush and Queen Anne's lace — a red, white and blue bouquet.

Three rafts were slid into the purling creek at the put-in place. We received instructions about safety, and a boatman held up a forty-foot nylon rope, a lifeline in case anyone was bounced out. (Exclamations of alarm, real or pretended!)

In fact, this was simply a fun ride, little more than an afternoon frolic on Class II rapids. But it was a novel experience to all the visitors, and they clutched the hand lines apprehensively.

It was delightful to drift through that beautiful countryside. Mount Earl Grey peaked to 9,000 feet, snowcapped but worn and older than the Rockies facing it across the East Kootenay Valley. We saw wide cleared paths where in winter skiers zoom downhill after first being raised by ski lifts. ("They are free in winter to skiers over sixty," I was informed with a significant smile.)

We successfully helped paddle through a canyon, through rapids named the Rock Garden and Pinball. We got splashed a little, and the girls screamed a little and held on with white knuckles.

We were on the river slightly more than one hour, and ended up under a bridge at the posh Panorama Hotel. Since a large part of its business is with skiers, the interconnecting corridors were very lightly populated in midsummer. I was the sole guest as the others returned to Radium, declaring they had had a wonderful time, and wishing it had lasted longer.

FOR FURTHER INFORMATION:

Glacier Raft Company
Box 219
Radium Hot Springs, British Columbia
Canada V0A 1M0
Phone (604) 347-9218

Kootenay River Runners
Box 81
Edgewater, British Columbia
Canada V0A 1E0
Phone (604) 347-9210

A raft filled with day trippers bounces down the gentle waves of Toby Creek.

18

Chilliwack River
BRITISH COLUMBIA

Rafting on the Chilliwack is the perfect example of catering to a large population close at hand. Three outfits, R.A.F.T., Hyak, and Whitewater Adventures, made this discovery in 1983. All were founded by energetic young Vancouverites. The latter two had learned from far-flung raft trips on the Firth and Nahanni that long trips, costly in transport, attracted well-heeled, adventurous clients — but not in sufficient numbers to be viable. The quick turnover at the south of the province helps to finance more daring ventures.

The broad valley of the lower Fraser is well-populated. It holds Vancouver, the largest city in the province though not its capital. Thus the rafting companies can draw upon a million Canadians in Greater Vancouver, only an hour's drive distant, to say nothing of the rest of the province and its visitors, including those from south of the border.

The Chilliwack River is not very long, but tumultuous enough in places. It drains Chilliwack Lake in the Cascade Mountains, less than five miles from the Washington state border. From there it dashes downhill thirty miles to Cultus Lake.

The city of Chilliwack lies sixty-two miles east of Vancouver, between the Trans-Canada Highway and the Fraser River, and the narrow valley of the Chilliwack lies to the southeast. Close at hand is the

Wetsuits *(top)* are supplied for rafting on the Chilliwack. Guests *(bottom)* wait to board a raft.

These Chilliwack rafters help themselves to lunch.

Whitewater carries one raft downstream while two others wait to head out.

There's always time to sunbathe on a gravel bar.

Skagit River Provincial Recreation Area, abutting Manning Provincial Park. Obviously this is an extremely popular area of "wilderness," crosshatched with trails. "Some six thousand people use the valley on an average day of a long weekend," said a park warden.

The Chilliwack is the most raftable whitewater within range of one- or two-day trips. The upper reaches plunge through gorges and race through canyons at speeds unsuitable for rafting. The rafts are put in below the canyon, which nevertheless provides a push. The season on this river is from the end of May to early September, with trips every day and especially on weekends.

Often groups of friends make this rafting a day's outing, and of course get the benefit of group rates.

The morning I was able to go, a group of hairdressers, mostly women in their twenties, stood around uncertainly. They and their boyfriends, all in full rafting costume, were timid about this novel entertainment and they stepped into the rafts quite gingerly. They made many merry comments about their own and their friends' appearance. Some looked svelte and lissome

Rafters frolic beneath a lovely cascade tumbling into the Chilliwack.

in black wetsuits. Others bulged. But the trip was made for just such a clientele.

Where we put in, the river was about ninety feet wide and full of mild rapids. "Lunch," Scotty announced in a couple of hours.

A veteran whitewater man, he soon had lunch makings spread on a gravel bank near a waterfall. (No one knew its name.)

When it came time to push on, one young man almost let his raft get away, and had to wade out after it. But we quickly hauled him back on board.

Scotty plied his long sweeps so nimbly we guests didn't have to use our paddles. The current and the oars carried us along with no effort on our part.

But the wetsuits were needed in the afternoon, when we encountered heavier rapids, especially the Tamahi, Sawmill and Campground rapids. We took on splashes of waves and bailed a bit. In the high waves of the Tamahi, I was bounced off my perch almost into Scotty's lap. The lad next to me leaned far forward into the well, making sure that if he were dislodged it would be into the raft, not overboard.

After Campground Rapids, where we hauled out, the river flattens and quietly enters Cultus Lake. We guests were transferred to the parking lot where the bus and our cars awaited us.

FOR FURTHER INFORMATION:

R.A.F.T. Inc.
Box 34051, Station "D"
Vancouver, British Columbia
Canada V6J 4M1
Phone (604) 261-RAFT
**   (800) 633-RAFT**

Hyak River Expeditions Inc.
1614 West 5th Avenue
Vancouver, British Columbia
Canada V6J 1N8
Phone (604) 734-8622

19

Skeena River
BRITISH COLUMBIA

John and Johnny Mikes (father and son) of Canadian River Expeditions, Vancouver, examine a detailed map of the upper Skeena.

By the time the Skeena River in central British Columbia joins the highway to Prince Rupert, it is a sober gray stream, wide and powerful. It has a mysterious atmosphere compounded of mist and distance and loneliness. The name, derived from K'shian, means "water of the clouds."

By comparison, the little-known upper Skeena is a wild, turbulent young river, smashing through black, rocky canyons. Boisterous waves churn through narrow gaps and around sharp bends.

That's why the 175 miles of upper Skeena are a rafter's delight. This river as well as other northwestern rivers was pioneered by "Big John" Mikes of Canadian River Expeditions of Vancouver. His son Johnny, twenty-seven, a chip off the old block for expertise and affability, met us at the Terrace airport. We sixteen guests and five boatmen had a rendezvous with a DC-3. John Mikes, formerly a Czech hotelier, was for a time gourmet chef at Banff Springs Hotel before the rafting bug bit him. He set the tone for all Canadian river rafting — a high standard of the best food available, superbly cooked, starting with appetizers of macadamia nuts and smoked salmon.

The DC-3 required two trips to move all of us and our gear, including three large rafts rolled up, tents and bedrolls, and a portable stove. We landed at Chipmunk Creek, a minor tributary of the Skeena, in a wide valley formed by low mountains.

We landed on an emergency service strip, a gravel run that had served railroad builders in 1859. For there, on the right-of-way, lay rusting rails and rotting ties of an abortive extension of the B.C. Railway. It was part of a projected extension from Fort St. James to Dease Lake via Telegraph Creek, 190 miles north. Work stopped when prudent minds realized that mining freight would never pay the upkeep, much less the millions of dollars already spent in construction. Only moose and bear lumber over the rails today.

We all fell to at once, packing our gear down to the edge of the young Skeena, milky green at this point. Johnny promised us plenty of whitewater in the next seven days.

No two rafting trips are ever the same, for much depends on the weather, the time of year, the water level and the company. So many of the Mikes' guests were repeaters that, when they clamored for a new river to run, he tracked down this one and laid on an extra trip in late summer. American guests who had rafted the notable Colorado and Snake rivers protested that they much preferred the isolation and remoteness of unblemished wilderness, and the total absence of other rafting parties.

Every rapid on the upper Skeena must be studied carefully in advance.

I should say that guests of the Mikes invariably leave the countryside as pristine as they found it. No tissues or tins, bottles or plastics remained to mark our passing.

"Soon we come to Peepee Rapids." There was a twinkle in Johnny's eyes.

"Why such a name?" we chorused.

"You'll see."

As we headed for the black shore, we could see the fast water foaming beyond. We all got out of the rafts to reconnoiter and choose a safe route through the billows. We scrambled over ledges and boulders washed smooth with centuries of scouring waters.

The canyon walls narrowed ahead and the river thundered between sheer cliffs, making a right turn out of sight. Spray shot up to us, and we had to shout our useless advice to the boatmen. Before heading back to rejoin our rafts, many felt a sudden urge to step behind a bush. Johnny grinned, "See, what did I tell you?"

We catapulted through the rapids in fine style, skillfully directed by each boatman. Just in time, each swung the raft with long oars past the rocks into the least turbulent current — except through the narrowest gap, where we had no choice but to take the roughest water. We got wet, but thought it all great for the adrenalin. We had donned slickers with our morning coffee, but now suddenly the sun shone hot and golden.

"Boy, that was neat!" exlaimed fourteen-year-old Tommie Sears from Seattle. "Let's do it again." But rafts go downstream only, not up.

Tommie was along with his grandmother, Emma Berger of Seattle. She was an ardent rafter, and took

85

Raft successfully navigates one of the Skeena's canyons.

Tommie with her on many trips into Canada. "Yeah," said Tommie, "she's really neat."

Oddly enough, Emma was our one casualty, the only one to get bounced overboard in a rapid. It's nothing too unusual, and not serious. Her life jacket of course held her up, and she didn't lose hold of the safety line strung around each raft. She was pulled aboard at once, and her raft nudged onto a tiny beach in the canyon. A couple of women held up a poncho for a curtain while Emma shed her soaking slacks and blouse and pulled on dry ones from her waterproof plastic sack. Emma kept on laughing, only her head bobbing above the curtain as if she were doing a striptease. She made it all so amusing that we almost wished we too had been dunked.

We found nice campsites at the confluences of small rivers — Mosque, Sustut and Babine — wide sandbars, with dense virgin forest crowding behind. Much of the time we spent floating through black shadowy canyons, not huge canyons as on some trips, but intimate. Although this was said to be one of the best areas in British Columbia for hunting and trapping, we observed little wildlife other than a porcupine and one otter. Once a black bear came sniffing downwind toward our campfire. Johnny scared it off with a couple of blasts from a gun fired into the air. The sound reverberated through the canyon and Bruin took to his heels. He was certainly in no danger from our group of conservationists.

And though the bald eagle may be an endangered species south of the border, where it is an emblem, it is certainly much in evidence along the upper Skeena. John Mikes had pointed out to his guests that if they wanted steelhead trout this was the country, but they would need a special steelhead permit. Nobody bothered. Few rafters are enthusiastic anglers, I've noticed.

Our topographical map showed the route of the Yukon Telegraph Line that linked the Klondike gold creeks with the outside world in 1898. The line was originally meant to run through Alaska and Siberia to reach Europe, and by 1867 stretched as far as Telegraph Creek on the Stikine. But then the Trans-Atlantic Cable was laid successfully, and this roundabout western project was dropped. The gold rush revived it, and the

Whitewater *(top)* almost obscures the lead raft as it seeks a route through a canyon. Another raft *(above)* plunges over easier rapids in one of the many black-walled canyons of the upper Skeena.

Cabin 4 *(top)* of the Overland Telegraph line sits, deserted, beside the Skeena. Glass bottles and other relics *(bottom left)* found in the abandoned cabin line up along an outside shelf. A few totem poles *(bottom right)* still stand at the Indian village at Kispiox.

A group picture ends the rafting trip on the upper Skeena.

line went through to Dawson City to carry news (and not least, stock market quotations) north and south.

The relay cabins were set thirty-two miles apart. The operators patrolled the line, especially when a falling tree knocked it out of service. In quiet off-hours, the winter-isolated linesmen played chess over the little-used line. Some of the old log cabins still stand, long outmoded. We came upon Cabin No. 4 perched on a high bank, still habitable in an emergency but showing its age. There was evidence of a small vegetable garden, and of a barely discernible swath through the bush where the single wire once ran.

We overlooked Cabin No. 3 on the right bank, but below pulled out on a level beach, a novelty after a series of black canyons. We had meant to look for the abandoned Indian village of Kuldo, but the trees dripped with rain and the bush looked too dense to penetrate, so we missed the opportunity to explore. Kuldo had been an important market for eulachon oil brought over the Grease Trail from the Nass River. This condiment was prized by the Tsimshian tribe.

Later we stopped at our first human settlement, Kispiox, an Indian totem pole village. Its tall poles have been collected into one area of the village and are now looked after as memorials of a once highly artistic Indian culture.

We were reaching the end of our 175-mile float at Hazelton, where we would meet a bus for Terrace, 85 miles down the now-broad Skeena.

"Any complaints?" asked Big John later.

"Yeah," said Tommie. "It should have been two or three days longer so we could explore. Otherwise, it was neat!"

We agreed.

20

Thompson River
BRITISH COLUMBIA

The South Thompson, a docile river given to lakelike expansions, drains the Shuswap Lake in the Okanagan Valley, finds a low threshold in the Monashee Mountains, and joins the more vigorous North Thompson at Kamloops. The two branches fuse and expand to form Kamloops Lake before draining westward as the Thompson River, some 500 miles total. From Kamloops to Lytton on the Fraser River tallies about 165 road miles.

Fur trader and explorer for the Northwest Company (rival to the Hudson's Bay Company), Simon Fraser believed he was following in the wake of David Thompson, who explored the Columbia from source to mouth. Fraser was wrong. He was on an entirely different river, one more northerly, a fierce river in places. He named this access river for "the prince of explorers," though David Thompson never set eyes on his river. In courtesy, when drawing his marvelous maps, Thompson gave the name Fraser to the mighty river that the younger man had discovered.

Fraser and Thompson rivers both rise near Yellowhead (Tete Juane) Pass, on the western edge of Jasper National Park. Both gallop down the flank of the Rockies.

The first raft on either river, apart from possible Indian transports, came with the arrival of the Overlanders in 1862. One hundred fifty settlers were on their way from Ontario to the gold creeks of the Cariboo District. They made up rafts from tall, straight jack pines. These unreliable bundles lashed together with rope were a far cry from today's buoyant neoprene tubes. Some Overlanders chose the Fraser, dreading the terrors that awaited them. Astonishingly, only one man drowned in the churning water. The others all reached their destination.

Among those that chose the Thompson was the Schubert family, with three children and a fourth imminent. The raft carried them through Hell's Gate and safely to Kamloops, where Baby No. Four arrived safely two days later.

I had driven often enough beside both Thompson and Fraser, appalled yet fascinated by their waves. Rafting down the Thompson in 1976 was my first experience in this zestful form of recreation. It was pleasurable in many ways — the landscape viewed from a novel angle, the congeniality of a group of strangers, the lasting friendships.

Dan Culver *(far left)*, owner/operator of Whitewater Adventures, Vancouver, rides down the Thompson. A raft *(right)* swirls through the Thompson's rapids.

Heavy rapids of the Thompson dwarf a raft in Pitquah Canyon.

It was also one of the earliest trips undertaken by Dan Culver's Whitewater Adventures of Vancouver. Our single raft consisted of two J-tubes — pontoons slightly upcurved in front, each twenty-two feet long, each consisting of four compartments inflated to three pounds pressure. The raft was army surplus material. All our camping gear went into individual waterproof bags, and camera gear into waterproof ammunition boxes. Each guest signed a statement absolving Whitewater Adventures from blame for accident or loss. What had I gotten myself into? I wondered.

We put in at Savona (accent on the first syllable), at the outlet of Kamloops Lake. At first a twenty horsepower engine nudged us along. The blue water, though cold, tempted some young guests to leap overboard and allow themselves to be towed along, a variation of water-skiing. Wearing a life jacket at all times on the water was one of the few rules imposed upon us, and it was rigorously obeyed.

When our river guide turned off the motor, our craft drifted, gyrated, slid along stern first. In fact, we let the current take us over.

The Thompson runs through the driest real estate in Canada, where the sun bakes the naked hillsides and little grows but sagebrush and cactus. Red-plated ponderosa pines rise singly. The crisp grass on the terraces provides pasture for cattle and, when irrigated, hay for the winter.

A stark reminder of the aridity of the valley is the sagging irrigation sluice that snakes along the hillsides on the south bank at the ghost town of Walhachin — so ghostly there's nothing else there.

At rest for the moment, small motor helps control raft in heavy rapids.

Once a group of Englishmen dreamed that the sunshine made the valley suitable for orchards. They were not necessarily wrong. They planted fruit trees, brought water miles from the river. Then in 1914, when it seemed their hopes would be realized, war broke out in Europe. To a man, the Englishmen put down spray guns and took up machine guns. They left the orchards to their wives' care, expecting to "be home by Christmas." Few of them survived, and the broken-down wooden aqueduct symbolizes the end of a dream.

After the Dry Belt we camped for the night on a tree-covered island, put up tents, built a fire. Everyone shared in the chores, and Sandy, the cook/partner, served the first of our tasty meals: artichokes, no less, a chocolate cake made in the Dutch oven, coffee and Australian wine.

In a happy mood we sat around the dying embers, listening to the surging waters, and watched six satellites hurrying in all directions across the dark sky. Closer to hand we could watch the two transcontinental railway lines snaking along on tracks on both sides of the river. When the lighted coaches entered one of the three snowsheds, they resembled huge glowworms. Although we had put up tents, everyone preferred to sleep under the stars.

Next morning we encountered the Thompson's real whitewater, though we had enjoyed the earlier rapids.

Our raft rode nicely, spray skimming over the bow. In heavy rapids, which we approached with due caution, big waves boiled up and over the sides of the raft while we clung tighter to the lashings and cheered. We made erratic twists, and it felt at times like a super

Plummeting waterfall and pool below Spences Bridge invite bathers.

roller-coaster ride. Big whirlpools sucked us in, spun us around a few times, then spewed us out. In fact, by use of the little motor, and the back current of the eddies, we sometimes floated back upstream to enjoy the fun of running the fast water all over again.

These violent actions lasted only seconds, whether in the rapids named Frog, the Cutting Board, the Devil's Cauldron, or, in the dramatic Pitquah Canyon, the spine-tingling Jaws of Death.

Cars and their riders paused at Spences Bridge to watch us hurtle by, perhaps predicting a dire fate for us, or perhaps envying us.

My own first rafting junket continued on the Fraser, through Hell's Gate and the sixty-mile canyon. About thirty-five miles of turbulent water romps between Spences Bridge and the end of the Thompson River. Rafters wanting only a short run of whitewater may take three hours on this stretch of the Thompson, arriving at Lytton, where the clear waters of the Thompson refuse to mingle with the muddy Fraser, and the two run side by side for nearly a mile before the Fraser silt wins.

Outfitters now offer a package deal. Guests may be picked up in Vancouver by bus on a Saturday morning, carried to a suitable put-in on the Thompson, fed handsomely, and returned to the city on Sunday afternoon — a splended mini-vacation.

FOR FURTHER INFORMATION:

Hyak River Expeditions Inc.
1614 West 5th Avenue
Vancouver, British Columbia
Canada V6J 1N8
Phone (604) 734-8622

Whitewater Adventures
1616 Duranleau Street
Granville Island
Vancouver, British Columbia
Canada V6H 3S4
Phone (604) 669-1100
(604) 689-RAFT

Chilcotin River
BRITISH COLUMBIA

The continuing act of creation is nowhere better demonstrated than along the swift rivers of central British Columbia. Rafting down the Chilko, Chilcotin and Fraser rivers for 260 miles provided a closeup on the changing landscape and its geology.

Dirt roads flank the rivers; paved highways keep a prudent distance from their tumultuous waves, where possible. All three are lonely rivers, shunned by boats, their shores almost empty of mankind.

To provide Canadians and their guests with river-scapes impossible from land, John Mikes of Canadian River Expeditions, Vancouver, makes this lengthy rafting trip available half-a-dozen times each summer. To boating and camping he adds a variety of transportation and an exciting ten-day vacation far from the bustle and crowds of daily life. In all our miles on the three rivers, we encountered few individuals and only one boat — the cable ferry at Big Bar, which serves ranches on the west side of the Fraser.

We actually made a circuit of some six hundred miles. A bus carried Mikes' guests up the Sunshine Coast to Bute Inlet, to meet a tug that carried us to the head of the lovely fjord. There an amphibious aircraft lifted us over the peaks and glaciers of the high Coast Range to set us down on Chilko Lake, a fifty-mile-long sapphire gouged out by glacial movement during the last ice age.

In a setting of gnarled Douglas firs and a backdrop of snowy peaks, we set up tents or slept under the stars with no fear of molestation — scarcely even mosquitoes. Our three large rafts were waiting, already inflated and virtually unsinkable. They rode the waves like the mergansers we overtook. Each carried eight guests and

Chilko Lake, fifty miles long, is the starting point of the Chilcotin trip.

Guests *(above)* sit on logs around a campfire beside Chilko Lake. Rafters *(above right)* paddle the riffles of the Chilko River.

an experienced boatman, who doubled as a gourmet cook. We had paddles for any who cared to use them, oars for the boatmen. A small motor for emergencies is mandatory in the Fraser Canyon.

Chilko Lake drains into Chilko River, its riffles a gentle introduction to the rapids we would meet later. We guests paddled four to a side until we approached Lava Canyon, a twenty-two-mile rift where the river froths over big boulders — too savage, John Mikes reckoned, for rafting. We were obliged to portage around it in a van. But the canyon can be run when the water level diminishes, Mikes decided in later runs.

At the foot of Lava Canyon the Taseko River foams in from the east. Here we set up camp under jack pines in a parklike setting. This was true Cariboo country, part of the Dry Belt of British Columbia, famous for its clear skies and sunny days. That night we had shish kebabs grilled over the campfire, and our boatmen proved themselves as proficient at camp cookery as at guiding us through the rapids.

The next day, one of the boatmen nearly came to grief at Siwash Bridge. Aiming at the gap between the pilings, he turned the raft too sharply. It was thrown against the rock wall, rubbed a bit, and tilted alarm-ingly before another wave washed it back into midstream.

This is the only bridge over the Chilko, but not the first. Bridges were rare before the coming of the white man, but used in the Chilcotin area. The Chilcotin Indians, traders and middlemen between the coast dwellers and the Shuswap tribe inland, found it conven-ient to build bridges over mountain streams too rocky for navigation.

Chilko River bent abruptly east, and presently a slim river entered from the west. This was the Chilcotin, rising in beaver meadows in the foothills of the Coast Range. Though narrower than our river, it was longer, and the Chilko lost its name to the Chilcotin. "The Chillacoot" is what the Indians and the old-timers call it. It means "young men's river."

All three rafts moved quickly through the cold green water, shooting, swerving, taking water over the splash-board, to the hilarity of the passengers though our feet and seats were soon drenched.

For some miles the banks of the Chilcotin are low and relatively flat, a broad alluvial plain where the gigantic block of glacial ice stagnated and dropped its silt. The result is superior rangeland. Ranching began

in the 1860s with Tom Hance from Illinois, and his descendants still live around Hanceville.

We tented that night in a meadow where ospreys perched on dead trees overlooking gravel bars, and nighthawks boomed at dusk. Beyond the grasslands we could see lights twinkling from the Anahim Creek Indian Reserve, as we feasted on barbecued pork chops picked up by arrangement at Alexis Creek.

Next day we negotiated the "goosenecks" of the Chilcotin, a rough, narrow winding stretch of the river, to its junction with Big Creek, a swift, cold stream tumbling in cascades from a glacier. It was a lovely campsite of evergreens and cottonwoods, and our first

act was to string up a clothesline to dry our wet socks, pants and shoes.

Rafting on turbulent rivers is great fun, spiced with an element of danger. When we entered two miles of rapids next morning, the boatmen yelled, "Hang on!" We did, but even so, two women were jolted into the seething river when their raft struck a submerged rock, buckled and flung them overboard. Their life jackets saved them from more than a dunking, for they were quickly rescued and dried off beside a big fire.

At Farwell Canyon, named for an early settler, the Chilcotin Forest Road offers a back door to the Gang Ranch, long the largest in Canada. An active sand dune

Guide Jim Lavalley *(left)* cuts thin slices of smoked salmon as appetizers, then clowns for the camera *(above)* with a helper.

97

High, steep banks *(left)* mark the arid country at the confluence of the Fraser and Chilcotin. Pulpit Rock *(below)* casts shadows on rafts floating down the Fraser.

near the north end of the bridge inches closer to the brink of the canyon walls with every wind that blows. This was always a very important salmon fishing site to the native Shuswap people. They tell a myth to explain the prehistoric blockage of the river. Coyote, a demigod, liked the Shuswaps and disliked the Chilcotins. He therefore made a dam across the river so the salmon could not gain the upper reaches, thus keeping all the salmon for his favorites. "Only recently,"

Boatmen cautiously approach the rapids of Farwell Canyon.

FOR FURTHER
INFORMATION:

Canadian River Expeditions, Ltd.
845 Chilco Street
Vancouver, British Columbia
Canada V6G 2R2
Phone (604) 738-4449

Thompson Guiding, Ltd.
Riske Creek, British Columbia
Canada V0L 1T0
Phone (604) 879-6710

they say, "has the river broken through the barrier."

It is probable that two fish ladders, above the bridge and now above the water level, had a great deal to do with restoring the salmon run. The Chilcotin is immensely valuable in that it spawns one-third of the Fraser's catch.

Below Farwell Canyon and its recent sand slide, we camped on a silty beach among small yellow cactus flowers and lavender sego lilies. A golden eagle soared above the gorge, and we saw silhouetted on the high benchlands a dozen California bighorn antelopes recently saved from extinction and now totally protected.

At Big John Canyon, named for our genial host John Mikes, the Chilcotin plunges off its plateau down to the level of the Fraser. A new rock slide had poured down the steep slopes at the narrowest part of the canyon,

changing the watercourse. Our rafts tied up where an eddy swept them ashore. Our boatmen climbed a rough ladder they had set up, and with the aid of a rope scrambled high enough up the sliding slope to reconnoiter and choose a new pathway through the next perilous stretch.

One hundred fifty miles from its source, the Chilcotin plunges into the muddy Fraser and the clear green tributary soon loses its identity.

In a way the Chilcotin might be deemed the parent of the Fraser. Geologists say that during the Pliocene period the Fraser flowed east into the Parsnip-Peace drainage system, and so to the Arctic Ocean. An earth barrier divided the two river systems. Then about two million years ago the Chilcotin broke through the divide and was captured by the Fraser. Since then it has flowed south to the Pacific.

Fraser River
BRITISH COLUMBIA

From its very inception on the west side of Yellowhead (Tete Juane) Pass, the Fraser is an impatient young giant. It sprawls like a gigantic meathook across the province of British Columbia, draining 92,000 square miles of mountain, plateau and valley. Milky with glacial silt, its infant leap changes to a crawl in the Rocky Mountain Trench.

At Prince George the Fraser right-angles south, where the Nechako adds to its adolescent ebullience and the Quesnel and Chilcotin rush in. Here the famous Fraser River Canyon may be said to begin, deep and at first broad, then narrowing to the 30 miles of rock walls to Hope. There it makes another right-angle to flow through a broad valley, where it slows down and drops silt to form fertile islands. It reaches salt water at Vancouver after 840 turbulent miles.

Green and glacially cold at its source, then muddied with clay and ground rock, its brown waves edged with ecru keep tearing at their confining banks, here uprooting a towering cottonwood, there bypassing a fish ladder, elsewhere precipitating a rock slide, and ceaselessly cutting a deeper bed until it levels off in the broad Fraser Valley.

Simon Fraser, fur trader and explorer, followed the river's length in 1808, believing he was in the 1806 wake of David Thompson on the Columbia. He was not displeased to discover this was a river new to mapmakers, but he was appalled at the savagery of the terrain. "This country is so wild — a place where no humans should venture . . ."

Long before he reached the canyon, Fraser had learned to study fast water before embarking on it. Of one two-mile rapid he confided to his journal:

Steep banks contracted the channel to 40 or 50 yards. This immense body of water passing through this space in a turbulent manner, forming gulfs (whirlpools) and cascades and making a tremendous noise and a forbidding appearance, to say nothing of the yawning lateral ravines . . .

When Fraser and his French-Canadian voyageurs reached the precipitous walls below Hell's Gate, they found they must portage everything except the canoes, which they cached. The only way around the roiled water was by a spiderweb of saplings the Indians had draped from the heights. Fraser's party, with all its gear,

Raft floats down the Fraser, through semi-arid ranchlands.

Above Lillooet *(top)* is a formation called Pulpit Rock. Guests *(bottom)* prepare to camp below the distinctive rock.

had to climb the shaky ladder of sticks bound with vines, where a moment's inattention could lose a man his load and his life. Fraser pushed on to the sea despite hostile Indians — and then had to retrace the painful route home. No wonder he gave up exploring.

Yet nowadays half-a-dozen outfits conduct raft trips there for pleasure!

Southwest of Williams Lake the Fraser bends westward to gather in the clear green Chilcotin. The clean water is soon swallowed by the turgid Fraser, and we had to replenish our drinking water at French Bar Creek where clean, potable water flowed into the Fraser.

Hundreds of hoodoos, stone needles capped with slate, stand beside the central section of the river. At Big Bar the ferryman grinned and offered us a ride

Rafters picnic by the long-abandoned Big Slide gold mine.

Bridge over the Fraser, west of Williams Lake, leads to ranches.

across the river on his free cable ferry. He told us the biggest excitement in his life was the sheep migration. Trucks carry thousands of sheep to grazing lands west of the Fraser. Then, come fall, they take them back home again. "Used to be quite a chore when the sheep had to hoof it both ways. And they didn't like the ferry."

On the right (west) bank of the river we spotted a well-built log house and barn, said to be a hundred years old, deserted. Almost opposite, equally abandoned, was the Big Slide gold mine millhouse and adit. The mine was opened in 1872 and worked with some success by Chinese immigrants for fifty years. The only access to it was by mule track, now grown over.

Below, the Fraser hurls itself into Moran Canyon, carving the chasm deeper year by year. Moran is "a miniature Grand Canyon," as one writer phrased it. Its sheer walls rise two thousand feet high, topped by sage and rabbitbush. As usual, we were briefed on the next day's rapids, their size, their perils. Now our apprehension grew, our fears increased, and adrenalin pumped through our veins.

This canyon is one of several locations on the Fraser earmarked by engineers for power development, when some energy crisis becomes more urgent than the value of the salmon fishery. A 700-foot dam at Moran would pond the river back for 150 miles, creating a narrow lake all the way to Quesnel, blotting out much fast

water, and drowning the hoodoos and Pulpit Rock, an impressive crag.

We could hear Moran's rapids long before we saw them. Then the rafts plunged into deep troughs, leaped buoyantly to crests, stood on end momentarily. We shouted in exhilaration, and one wit roared, "Stop the raft. I want to get off."

"You can't," the boatman shouted back, deadpan. "You booked for the whole trip."

As we neared Lillooet, on its baked benchland by the river, we ended a long, thrilling slide of 260 miles from Chilko Lake, having dropped 3,000 feet in the process.

Now in calmer waters, we spun gently in eddies. In one, an eight-foot sturgeon thrust half its body out of the water, then quickly submerged. Sturgeon up to half a ton have been taken here, we were informed. Across the river, Indians tied themselves to rocks on shore in the traditional way, to dipnet for salmon.

Many Chinese immigrants were attracted to the gold in Cariboo creeks and Fraser gravel bars in 1858. They panned diligently and found some gold, but they were the scorn of their white neighbors when they insisted on sending boulders downriver for shipment to China. But these boulders were not mere ballast. They were jade of good value, though not the highest quality, infinitely more precious in China than gold nuggets.

Avalanche sheds *(left)* of the railway are across the Fraser Canyon from campsite. Sunglasses *(above)* of a young rafter reflect a nearby raft.

There is still plenty of jade beside the river, but it takes sharper eyes than ours to recognize it. We saw only rocks streaked with mud.

Some sixty-five miles below Lillooet, the Thompson flows in from the east at Lytton. We who had previously rafted the Thompson were now to attempt the magnificently sinister trough below Hell's Gate. At Boston Bar, Dan Culver added two extra pontoons to our raft for stability and an extra motor for power in the seething maelstrom ahead of us.

He could recall a raft that had come to grief here in 1979, drowning three men and stranding eight other passengers. By chance, Dan happened to be leading a flotilla of four rafts when he saw two men wave him down. He put his passengers ashore and rescued the two drenched survivors, then went on to rescue two more. Another outfitter rescued the one woman passenger, who had clung to the wrecked raft and been swept through Hell's Gate.

How had the accident happened? We wanted to know. Actually, the party of eleven had made the run successfully, and were repeating it for pictures. The raft had struck a rock and damaged the hinge of a pontoon, so it became unbalanced and flipped everyone into the fierce waves. This was the first fatal accident in rafting the Thompson-Fraser run.

An extra pair of pontoons is lashed to the raft before entering Hell's Gate on the Fraser River.

Since then rafting outfits have proliferated on the popular run, to the point where familiarity may breed contempt and first-time guests become overconfident, relying on the mandatory life jackets.

On a day trip in 1984 I encountered a freak accident in Hell's Gate. The raft capsized when it struck a whirl-pool — a huge hydraulic — and a following wave hit from behind. The raft sandwiched and tipped, dumping its sixteen passengers into the cauldron. The raft promptly righted itself. The boatman caught the hand line and helped people back on board, including three children of one family. The eddy pushed the raft against the rock wall, and some frightened passengers scram-bled onto a rock ledge.

Fortunately a man on top witnessed the accident, and ran to a couple of maintenance men at the terminus of the AirTram for help. They swiftly found ropes to dangle down the 130-foot cliff, and lifted three stranded rafters to the top. The boatmen meanwhile inched the raft close to the cliff, and got the rest aboard. The raft then maneuvered through the fast water until it could be beached. The final guest was carried farther down-stream and had to be rescued by helicopter.

No one suffered more than bruises and shaken nerves. Some viewed it all as adventure with the very real danger adding spice.

The Fraser is still a power to be reckoned with.

Though one episode was in the past and the second in the future, we were glad for the extra pontoons and motor.

Above us stretched the cables of the unique car ferry that carries automobiles and small trucks high above the swift river. Beyond was the Alexandra Bridge by which the railway spanned the river.

A small footbridge crosses Hell's Gate, the narrowest spot in the river, pinched in by road-building and a cliff collapse long ago. It is further narrowed by fish ladders on both sides, so migrating salmon can surmount the fierce surge in easy stages. All of us trooped ashore to visit the small museum and souvenir

Hell's Gate *(left)* is the narrowest, most tumultuous section of the Fraser Canyon. Fishladder was built jointly by the United States and Canada. A raft struggles *(right)* through Hell's Gate's tumultuous waves.

shop at the foot of the AirTram, whose two gondolas carry passengers to and from the Trans-Canada Highway. Since the Fraser was not too silted by recent rains, we could look down through the gratings and see the silvery fish resting in the pool-steps below. These and other fishways were built jointly by the United States and Canada, since both share the Fraser River salmon run.

Our boatman stood at the railing, studying the cauldron below, for the water level changes almost daily. At this time the surface was only twenty feet above normal, though the range can be as much as ninety feet. When the water is high rafting is forbidden as too dangerous. We were excited as we donned water-proof clothing for the chute through Hell's Gate, the climax of our trip. Dan made a final check, to make sure nothing could be sloshed overboard when we flashed through the tumultuous waters at a speed of twenty feet per second.

We entered the smooth V formed by the waters narrowing for the Gate. Now there was no turning back, no changing our minds. Our raft was flung into the cauldron of churning waves and slued around in the current; solid water shot over us. We were through Hell's Gate in seconds. The raft bounced up, shedding water.

Yet the river spirits had not released us. Immediately beyond were formidable whirlpools. We were sucked into one helplessly, so the raft buckled as it spun around several feet below the rim of the vortex. The thick plywood floorboards split under the strain.

Then centrifugal force spit us out again. It had all been very fast. We didn't have time to envisage our possible dire fate before we were sidelined and into the walled trench that Simon Fraser dared not canoe. Some fierce and wonderful rapids waited farther down, but they seemed anticlimactic by comparison.

At historic Yale, long head of navigation on the Fraser, the river breaks through the last mountain barrier and the canyon walls step back. Here we saw a few more Indians fishing, one of them an acquaintance of Dan's. By law the Indian could take as many fish as he wanted, but not for sale. Dan arranged a trade, and everyone was satisfied.

While Sandy dressed the salmon and swathed it in foil, we wandered the bank and discovered an overgrown corduroy road, the decayed remnants of the old Cariboo Wagon Road built in 1862 to the gold diggings up the Fraser. We raided a derelict farm for apples and greengage plums and the lane for ripe blackberries to make a banquet.

Replete and relaxed, we sat around our last campfire in a reminiscent mood. Dan spoke of his early rafting on the upper Fraser above Quesnel, and of his plans for the future. More rafting on more rivers. Farther away. Maybe the Chilcotin. Maybe even the Nahanni . . .

"Oh-h-h!" Our eyes were full of waking dreams, and we all felt a pang of reluctance to abandon this lovely life of roaring water and silent nights and days of unpeopled panoramas.

"Next year," we half promised one another. "Next year . . ."

FOR FURTHER INFORMATION:

Canadian River Expeditions, Ltd.
845 Chilco Street
Vancouver, British Columbia
Canada V6G 2R2
Phone (604) 738-4449

Kumsheen Raft Adventure Ltd.
Main Street
Lytton, British Columbia
Canada V0K 1Z0
Phone (604) 455-2296

Thompson Guiding, Ltd.
Riske Creek, British Columbia
Canada V0L 1T0
Phone (604) 659-5635

Whitewater Adventures
1616 Duranleau Street
Granville Island
Vancouver, British Columbia
Canada V6H 3S4
Phone (604) 879-6701

Index

Swans, trumpeter, 65
Sweeps, 45, 73, 82

T

Takhanne River, 67
Tamahi, 83
Taseko River, 96
Tatshenshini River, 41
Tatshenshini-Alsek, 69
Telegraph Creek, 84, 87
Terrace, 84, 89
Tete Jaune Pass, 90, 100
The Dangerous River, 60
Third Canyon, 59
Third, Charlie, 51, 53
Thompson, David, 90, 100
Thompson Guiding, Ltd., 99, 107
Thompson River, 90-94, 104
Thompson-Fraser run, 104
Three Rock Rapids, 2
Thrush, hermit, 27
Thunder Bay, 73
Toaster, 22
Toby Creek, 77, 79-80
Toby Lake, 79

Toiletbowl, 13
Toronto, 15, 20
Totem poles, 88, 89
Trans-Atlantic Cable, 87
Trans-Canada Highway, 72, 81, 107
Trilliums, 23
Trois Roches, 2, 3
Trout, 50
Tsimshian tribe, 89

U

UNESCO Heritage Property, 59
UNESCO World Heritage Property, 36
United Nations Heritage Properties, 54-55
United States, 107

V

van Pelt, Anne, 45
van Pelt, Jacques, 43, 46
Vancouver, 54, 61, 62, 64, 81, 84, 90, 94, 95
Videotapes, 7
Violets, 76
Virginia Falls, 41, 55, 57, 58

Volleyball, 17
Voyageurs, 5, 15, 44, 51, 100

W

Walhachin, 92-93
Walker Glacier, 68
Walleye, 26, 27
Washing Machine, vii, 7
Washington state, 81
Water, drinking, 102
Water fights, 7
Water ouzels, 67
Water slides, 43
Waterfall, 77, 83, 94
Watson Lake, 54, 60
Wetsuits, 3, 13, 16, 17, 22, 81
Wheelies, 23
Whirlpools, 94, 105
Whitefish, 46
Whitehorse, 62
Whitewater Adventures of Vancouver, 54, 81, 90, 92, 94, 107
Whooping cranes, 46, 47
Wilderness Encounters, 36
Wilderness Tours, 9, 14, 16, 18

Williams, Mike, 72, 73, 74
Williams Lake, 102, 103
Willow herb, 63
Wind-surfing, 17
Wine, Australian, 93
Winnipeg, 27
Winnipeg International Airfield, 24
Wolf, 59
Wolf, Arctic, 64
Wolf tracks, 56
Wood Buffalo National Park, 46, 47
World War I, 93
World War II, vi

Y

Ya-ha-tinda Ranch, 39
Yale, 107
Yellowhead Pass, 90, 100
Yellowknife, 47, 48
Yoho National Park, 72
Yukon, 43, 66-69
Yukon Telegraph Line, 87
Yukon Territory, 41, 54, 61-69